IN THE LOBSTER CAPITAL OF THE WORLD

DON HANNAH

July 90
Toronto.

For my darling, darling
John — who always
makes me feel like
a million, and
who writes like a
dream.

A.F.A.

xo
Don

Playwrights Canada Press
Toronto

PLAYWRIGHTS CANADA PRESS is the imprint of
PLAYWRIGHTS UNION OF CANADA
54 Wolseley Street, 2nd Floor
Toronto, Ontario, Canada M5T 1A5
Phone (416) 947–0201

PLAYWRIGHTS UNION OF CANADA operates with generous assistance from
the Canada Council, the Department of External Affairs, the Ontario Ministry of
Culture and Communications, the Ontario Arts Council, Alberta Culture, Alberta
Foundation for the Literary Arts, the Municipality of Metropolitan
Toronto—Cultural Affairs Division, and the City of Toronto through the Toronto
Arts Council.

Front cover photo by Michael Cooper.
Front cover design by Tony Hamill.
Editor: Tony Hamill.

Canadian Cataloguing in Publication Data
Hannah, Don, 1951-
    In the lobster capital of the world

A play.
ISBN 0–88754–490–8

I. Title.

PS8565.A515 1990   C812'.54   C90–093132-9
PR9199.3.H36I5 1990

First Edition: July 1990
Printed and bound in Canada

IN THE LOBSTER
CAPITAL OF THE WORLD

In the Lobster Capital of the World was first presented by Tarragon Theatre, Toronto on April 12, 1988 with the following cast:

EMMA	*Doris Petrie*
EDWARD	*Brian Torpe*
MICHAEL	*Donald Adams*
PATRICIA	*Nancy Beatty*
DAVID	*Ross Manson*

Directed by Andy McKim.
Sets were designed by Sue LePage.
Lighting by Louise Guinand.
Costumes by Melanie Huston.

The playwright thanks Tarragon Theatre and The Canada Council for their support during the writing of this play. Thanks also to Urjo Kareda, Andy McKim, Ken Garnhum and the May sisters.

The Characters

EMMA, *age 75, smart, warm and opinionated.*

EDWARD, *her oldest son, late thirties, good looking, gregarious, and very urban.*

MICHAEL, *her youngest son, mid thirties, quiet, withdrawn.*

PAT, *late thirties, smart, plain and down to earth.*

DAVID, *age 22, very slim, very sexy, very art school.*

The Setting

The play is set in a small town on the coast of New Brunswick in July.

The set has playing areas for the beach and for Emma's house. It should be as simple and minimal as possible, although there must be a sense of the presence of the house. Action is continuous—there are no breaks from scene to scene.

IN THE LOBSTER CAPITAL OF THE WORLD
is for Scott and Louise.

Act One

_____

On the beach, just before dawn, EMMA *is
walking, shining a flashlight on the sand in
front of her feet. She carries a plastic
shopping bag with a coffee thermos inside.
There is only the sound of waves. She stops.*

EMMA   There were five old crows in the yard this
morning—five of the darn things cawin' away when I
left the house. And I'm not lyin', they were as big as
dogs, as big as that yappy Pekingese of your mother's.
Never used to be crows around the house, never on
God's green earth. They're a deep forest bird. Same as
a jay.

    EMMA *starts to walk again. She stops.*

Both the boys are back at the house. I looked into their
rooms when I got up. They're sleeping like
babies...You know what I wish? I wish it was
1956...Real swift thinkin' that.

    EMMA *sighs and continues her walk.
Darkness. Thunder rumbles in the distance.*

> EMMA's *house, late evening. A summer*
> *storm with thunder, lightning and rain.*
> EDWARD *and* MICHAEL *sit in the*
> *sunporch.* EDWARD *is watching the rain,*
> MICHAEL *sits, head down, staring at his*
> *feet.* EDWARD *has cabin fever.* MICHAEL
> *would rather sit than talk.* EMMA *enters.*

EMMA   So, you boys all caught up yet?

> MICHAEL *groans.*

EDWARD   Where's the tape machine?

> MICHAEL *groans louder.*

EMMA   You had it last.

MICHAEL   Oh, don't start playin' any more friggin' opera.

EMMA   Let's just sit and listen to the rain for a spell.

MICHAEL   Don't they have headphones in Toronto?

EDWARD   Headphones drive me nuts.

MICHAEL   Yeah, well guess what drives me friggin' nuts?

EMMA   Michael, don't be like that.

> *Pause.* EMMA *takes an orange from her*
> *pocket. She holds it up. Both her sons look at*
> *it.*

EMMA   "It was a dark and stormy night."

EDWARD   Oh, no.

EMMA   Come on. "It was a dark and stormy night."

              EMMA *tosses the orange to* EDWARD *who*
              catches it.

EDWARD   Right.

EMMA   Come on, you wanted something to do, so let's play a
              little game.

EDWARD   (*sighing*) "It was a dark and stormy night and...it was
              hard to see."

              EDWARD *fakes tossing the orange to*
              MICHAEL, *then throws it back to* EMMA.

EMMA   (*catching it*) Oh! Oh you're bad. "It was a dark and
              stormy night, and it was hard to see and...and
              somewhere on the Old Shore Road..."

              EMMA *tosses the orange to* MICHAEL *who*
              bats it towards EDWARD.

EMMA   Oh, come on and play.

MICHAEL   I forget how.

EMMA   Get on with ya. If the stupid Old Girl can remember
              than surely someone as young and bright as you can
              remember, too. "It was a dark and stormy night and it
              was hard to see and somewhere—"

              EDWARD *tosses the orange to* MICHAEL
              but he doesn't move to catch it. It bounces off
              him and rolls on the floor.

MICHAEL   Waste a stupid time.

EDWARD   Unlike anything else we've been able to do all
         week...where'd that game come from anyway?

EMMA   It didn't come from anywhere. You kids made it up.

         Lightning, a very bright flash.

EDWARD   Whoa!

EMMA   Thousand and one, thousand and two, thousand and
         three, thousand and four, thousand and—

         Very loud thunder sounds.

EMMA   That's gettin' closer, just over four miles. Storm's
         probably at Jake's Corner. Must be ruining those glads
         that Muriel has in her front bed.

EDWARD   Which one's Muriel?

EMMA   Which one's Muriel? Muriel's the twin!

EDWARD   Oh I know that. I meant which twin.

EMMA   There's only one twin. Maudy died of hit and run ten
         years ago walking home from Chapter one night. Your
         father offered to give her a ride but she wouldn't take
         it. You know what they could be like. If she weren't
         such a jackass she'd be alive today.

         MICHAEL *groans. Pause. More lightning.*

EMMA   Just look at that miserable weather. And poor Muriel
         just worships those flowers.

         Thunder sounds.

EMMA   Was that closer?

> EDWARD *shrugs and bends to pick up the*
> *orange. But* MICHAEL *kicks it away.*

MICHAEL   Too late there, Stupid Face.

EDWARD   Aren't you a success story. (*pausing*) Anyone want a
            coffee?

EMMA   Oh, don't go playing with appliances in an electrical
            storm.

> EDWARD *starts to exit.*

EMMA   Wait for a while.

EDWARD   I'm going to make a phone call.

EMMA   Oh. Are you going to try to phone that friend of yours
            in Toronto again?

EDWARD   Is there a rule against it?

EMMA   No. None of my beeswax.

> EDWARD *exits. Pause, then* MICHAEL
> *stands up.*

EMMA   Where are you going?

MICHAEL   Crazy, you wanna come?

EMMA   Do you know who this friend is?

> MICHAEL *sighs, looks out at the rain.*

EMMA   It was just a little question.

MICHAEL   Well, how the hell should I know? Ask him if you
            wanna know so bad.

EMMA   Oh, he'd just think I was being a nosey old mother.

      Lightning flashes, a pause, then thunder
      sounds further away.

EMMA   Just look at that weather. Ed's not going to hang
      around here with weather like this—he'll catch the
      first plane back to Toronto. Darn rain. Last summer it
      was wind, the year before that it was cold. Won't we
      ever have summers again like we had when I was a
      girl? We haven't had a beach day in three years...I
      haven't been on a picnic in five.

MICHAEL Oh, you're nuts. We went on a picnic when your crazy
      brother was here in June.

EMMA   You're right. I take that back. I'm sorry, you're right.
      The weather was nice that day for once...I just never
      saw so many flies! Remember the flies?...Can't you
      remember the flies?

MICHAEL No, I can't remember the flies.

EMMA   Oh, Mikie, they were like crows! Great big buggers.
      Swarms of them. Oh, you do remember cause you
      went and sat in the car with the windows up. Told me
      yourself you were getting away from the flies.

MICHAEL I was getting away from you.

EMMA   You're big brother isn't mean to me like you are, you
      know.

MICHAEL That's cause he's only been here for a week.

EMMA   Poor you. You may as well live on the moon for all I
      see of you. No one's asking you to stay down here,
      you know. You could leave the poor old Maritimes,
      just like everyone else.

MICHAEL   And you'd be just fine down here on your own.

EMMA   Maybe I would. Maybe I just would.

MICHAEL   Oh, you're crazy.

EMMA   Not half as crazy as you must be, living down here in the sticks with a stupid old woman.

            EDWARD *returns.*

EMMA   Boy, that was quick. Your friend must be one fast talker.

EDWARD   He isn't home.

EMMA   Oh. Out a lot, isn't he? (*pausing*) Would you like something sweet?

EDWARD   No.

EMMA   There's date squares in the pantry.

            EDWARD *shakes his head.*

EMMA   Or if you'd like to take a look, I think you'll find a few molasses cookies in the freezer.

EDWARD   No, I don't like those molasses cookies much.

EMMA   Well, for your information, these aren't mine, they're the ones you like. They're your father's.

EDWARD   God, how old are they?

EMMA   Just last fall. They're perfectly fine. They're frozen. We put them in about a week before he went to the hospital. There's not a thing wrong with them.

EDWARD   Jesus Murphy.

EMMA   What did you want me to do? Throw them out
because he passed away?

EDWARD   No, but you could have eaten them.

EMMA   You like them more than Mike and I do. We saved
them for you...would you toss me that old shawl?

> EDWARD *gives her a shawl that is draped
> over the back of a chair.*

EMMA   Thank you very kindly...The old Indian says there's
gonna be deep snows this year in October! I never
saw such miserable weather in my life.

> *There is a faint flash of lightning.*

EMMA   Storm's moving out to the Strait. (*pausing*) Sure is
different without Dad around, isn't it? Not the same
old place at all. (*pausing*) Oh, did I tell you that old
Roweena passed away in the spring? In Florida?

EDWARD   Yes, you did.

EMMA   The notice in the paper said that she was seventy-one
but that's a lie. She was a good five years older than
me at least. Went to the mall there one day and keeled
over at the check-out. They say she was dead before
she even hit the floor. That's the way to go, boys oh
boys, fine one day and with your Maker the next.
None of this hangin' on. That's three since Christmas:
Roweena, Verna and old June.

EDWARD   God, don't you know anybody who's still alive?

EMMA   We're all fading pretty fast. Before you know it, I'm
going to be the only English female left in this neck of

EMMA	the woods. I even miss old Roweena every once in a while.
EDWARD	Oh, you'll find someone new to crab about.
EMMA	Anybody new here has no time for me—they all parlez-vous the ding dong.
EDWARD	Don't start up on that stuff again, please.
EMMA	Well, you don't live here, you don't know what it's like. Does he Mike?
MICHAEL	Oh, be quiet.
EMMA	Don't tell me to be quiet, I'm your mother.

MICHAEL *groans.*

EMMA	It's not the same little town it used to be. English and French used to get along when I was a kid. We lived together side by side with no problems. If you'd stay here a while you'd know what I was talking about. I don't know whose kid you are, traipsing off to Ontario. Although I understand there's nothing here for you—no art galleries round these parts. Least ones that aren't Acadian. No one loves the Maritimes more than I do, but it's no place for young people, especially English young people. No reason for you to ever come back here except to see the poor Old Girl on her birthday.
MICHAEL	Anyone ever tell you you're a pain in the neck?
EMMA	Yes, many times. You certainly aren't the first, Boy.
EDWARD	Look, by the way. Patsy phoned me from Edmonton just before I came down, and she's going to be in

EDWARD   Rexton visiting her Mom in a few days. She said
                she'd like to come down and see everybody. If that's
                okay...with everybody.

                EMMA *and* EDWARD *both look at*
                MICHAEL.

EDWARD   Mike, she said that if you thought it was a bad idea,
                she wouldn't come. I could just borrow Mom's car
                and go up there.

MICHAEL   I don't care.

EDWARD   Which? If I go up there or if she comes down here?

MICHAEL   Either one. Doesn't matter to me.

EDWARD   You're sure?

MICHAEL   Yes, I'm sure.

EDWARD   Because, you know, don't say "yes" if you don't mean
                it.

MICHAEL   I said I didn't friggin' care.

EDWARD   I just wanted to make sure, that's all.

MICHAEL   So you made sure, Stupid Face.

EDWARD   Look, I just asked you to tell me how you feel.

MICHAEL   And I said I didn't give a shit! Christ Almighty, you
                want me to sign a stupid affidavit?

EDWARD   No, I just wanted to make sure, that's all.

MICHAEL   So you made sure.

EMMA   (*pausing*) Michael dear, are you really sure?

MICHAEL   Jesus H. Christ, get off my friggin' back, will ya?

            MICHAEL *exits*.

EMMA   I always set him off.

EDWARD   No you don't. He sets himself off.

EMMA   Well, Edward, she was his wife. Even if the marriage
            only did last a week.

EDWARD   But that was almost fifteen years ago!

EMMA   Yes, well, and a lot has happened to you in those years.

EDWARD   Oh, and nothing's happened to him?

EMMA   You're looking at the last person on earth who'd
            know. I wish you'd spend some time with him, have a
            little talk. Why don't you go out and spend a couple of
            days with him at his camp? I think he'd really like that.

EDWARD   The last time I went out to that shack in the woods we
            had to sit around on car seats from Aunt Jane's old
            Chev—you could still smell her cats on them. And he
            was sleeping on that ratty old mattress she died on. It
            was like a weekend in Dogpatch.

EMMA   That was ages ago. Now he's worked darn hard on
            that camp of his and it wouldn't hurt you to make the
            effort.

EDWARD   Why don't you go?

EMMA   I'd look some cute wading the Goshen River with an
            overnight case on my head.

EDWARD	You mean he hasn't finished the road yet?
EMMA	He'll never finish it as long as I'm livin'. He does need a place to get away from the Old Girl, you know.
EDWARD	Does he ever go out with anybody? Does he date?
EMMA	Your guess is as good as mine. He doesn't talk.
EDWARD	Well, you should be used to it—Dad was just the same.
EMMA	He was not! He talked to me. Cripes Kate, neither one of you ever talked to the other—and I was the big fool in the middle. But I do wish you would try and communicate with your own brother. Is that too much to ask? It wouldn't hurt you to try.
EDWARD	I have tried! I have tried and half the time he doesn't even talk at all. When he came to Toronto it drove me nuts. Didn't want to do anything—go out or anything—just sit in the kitchen. Days I had to go to work he'd turn up at the gallery ten minutes after I opened and he'd just stand there, grunt if you tried to talk. And if anyone else came in, he'd have to go hide in the back room.
EMMA	You boys were both shy.
EDWARD	Shy! My friend Joan had us over for dinner and he spent the whole evening in her bathroom, reading magazines. We waited over an hour for him before she could serve dessert. He's not shy, he's rude.
EMMA	But don't you think you could draw things out of him?
EDWARD	Like what? I couldn't even get him to tell me if he was hungry. "Do you want to go eat?" (*shrugs, grunts*) "Want to go out for a drink?" (*shrugs, grunts*) "Go for a walk?" (*shrugs, grunts*) Everything I asked

EDWARD   him it was (*shrugs, grunts three times*) Jesus Murphy, drove me nuts! And it's not that I don't like Michael, or that I don't care, it's just that I know it's pointless, you know? Pointless with Dad, pointless with Mike, just pointless.

EMMA   Suit yourself...Mike and his father used to talk, you know, every little once in a while they'd have a little talk. Mostly about the darn fools they worked with down in that office, or hockey. But I heard him talk to your father about that trip to Toronto to see you, and do you know what he said?

EDWARD   Oh, he probably said it was the best trip he ever had in his life.

EMMA   That's right. Those were his words exactly.

EDWARD   Well then, his worst trip must have been a real doozer. Where do you suppose he went for that one?

EMMA   Vermont, for his honeymoon.

EDWARD   Oh.

EMMA   You know Patsy called me from Edmonton after your father died.

EDWARD   Yes, she told me.

EMMA   We had a long talk—must have cost the kid a fortune. It meant a great deal to me because your father meant so much to her.

EDWARD   I know.

EMMA   Now, whatever happened between her and your brother—I don't know. I don't know and it's none of my business. And I can't say whether it would be a

EMMA   good thing for him to see her or not. He was never here when she came to visit your father and me. If it was just me, she could stay the whole summer, like old times when she and you were kids in university. But it's not up to me, it's up to Michael.

EDWARD   Right.

EMMA   It's darn hard for some people to talk about what really matters. You should know that.

   EMMA *picks up the orange and exits.*

> *The rain has stopped.* EDWARD *joins*
> MICHAEL *outside the house. It is very late at*
> *night. They sit in lawnchairs.* MICHAEL
> *takes a joint out of his pocket.*

MICHAEL   She go to bed?

EDWARD   Yeah. A while ago.

> MICHAEL *lights the joint.*

EDWARD   Homegrown?

> MICHAEL *barely nods.*

EDWARD   At the camp?

> MICHAEL *grunts.*

EDWARD   At the camp?

> MICHAEL *doesn't react.*

EDWARD   Did you grow it at the camp?

MICHAEL   No, I grow it down in the park on friggin' Main Street.

EDWARD   Sorry I asked.

> MICHAEL *passes* EDWARD *the joint.*
> EDWARD *tokes.*

EDWARD   Jeeze, that's rough.

MICHAEL   It works.

> MICHAEL *takes the joint back, tokes, them*
> *passes it to* EDWARD *who shakes his head.*
> MICHAEL *shrugs and finishes it.*

EDWARD   I went for a walk today, before the rain. (*pausing*)
Went walking all over town.

MICHAEL   Wow.

EDWARD   Anyone ever tell you you're hopeless?

> *Pause.*

MICHAEL   So, you went for a walk.

EDWARD   Yeah.

> *Pause.*

MICHAEL   Was it fabulous?

EDWARD   No...It was weird. (*pausing*) I walked through the
park.

MICHAEL   What's left of it.

EDWARD   (*pausing*) You know those guys that hang out on the
park bench near the street? They look just the same as
the tribe that hung out there thirty years ago. I had this
flash of panic when I went by that some fifteen-year
old would try to beat me up.

MICHAEL   Aren't you swift.

EDWARD   Oh, dry up. Remember all those jerks? Moose
Melanson, Dink Estabrooks, and that one that was
always with them, you know, Squash Pie was his old
man. What was his name?

MICHAEL   Squash Pie's kid?

EDWARD   Yeah.

MICHAEL   That's a real hard one, Stupid Face.

EDWARD   Why, what was it?

MICHAEL   Little Squash Pie.

EDWARD   Oh. (*pausing*) What about Hop Hebert. He still around?

MICHAEL   Hop Hebert? How the hell would I know?

EDWARD   He got married, didn't he?

MICHAEL   How stupid do you get?

EDWARD   (*imitating*) "I don't live here, I don't know."

MICHAEL   Hop's old wife has been calling the cops on him for twenty-five friggin' years. Last winter she found out he was screwing around with her sister and she went at him with an axe. Only he's such a friggin' lard ass it just bounced off.

EDWARD   You know, when I was a kid I thought he was a really good-looking guy.

MICHAEL   Hop!

EDWARD   Yeah, Hop. What's he look like now?

MICHAEL   I don't know, I'm not gay. (*pausing*) He looks like shit. You know Elvis Presley when he died? That's Hop on a good day.

EDWARD   What a waste.

MICHAEL   Oh, yeah, he should have been a fashion model or something.

EDWARD   That's not what I meant.

MICHAEL   Nuclear scientist.

EDWARD   Alright.

MICHAEL   Movie star brain surgeon.

EDWARD   Why do I even try to talk to you?

      Pause.

MICHAEL   So, you walked around town looking for Hop Hebert?

EDWARD   I just said I went out for a walk, that's all. (*pausing*) They're setting up the Ferris wheel for the Lobster Carnival. I watched them when I went down to the shore. It was all lit up and going around with no music. Then I walked along the beach—smelled the salt air, listened to the waves.

MICHAEL   You love this dump so much how come you only come home one week a year?

EDWARD   You hate it so much how come you stay for fifty-two? (*pausing*) Mike, you know Floyd?

MICHAEL   No.

EDWARD   Yes, you do.

MICHAEL   Alright, I do. Who the hell is he?

EDWARD   He used to be my partner at the gallery.

MICHAEL   Oh, now we're back in friggin' Toronto! Sorry, I
            thought you were still in this dump walkin' along the
            beach. Smelling the fabulous salt air, watching our
            fabulous waves.

EDWARD   Christ.

MICHAEL   So did that jerk drag home another art deco lamp or
            something?

EDWARD   Forget it. (*pausing*) Pointless.

            Pause.

MICHAEL   I cut down the tree by the clothes pole.

EDWARD   Wow.

MICHAEL   (*pausing*) It was old and rotten.

EDWARD   (*pausing*) It was home base for hide and seek,
            remember?

MICHAEL   (*shrugging*) I never played, I was too little. (*pausing*)
            You were always the last one to get caught.

EDWARD   Thought you never played, Stupid Face.

MICHAEL   I watched. Mom thought I was asleep but I was
            watching you play from my bedroom window.

EDWARD   Only game I was ever any good at. I'd be lying over
            there in a hole by the corner of the lilacs while it got
            darker and everybody'd be standing around that tree
            calling for me. What was that? "Save the..." No.

MICHAEL   "Free the bunch."

EDWARD   Right. "Free the bunch...Eddie Eddie, free the
            bunch." (*pausing*) You get a birthday present yet for
            Mom?

MICHAEL   No, you?

EDWARD   Is there anything that she needs? Something for the
            kitchen?

MICHAEL   Like another appliance? Another yogurt maker?
            Maybe a Dust Buster this time.

EDWARD   She said she wanted the yogurt maker.

MICHAEL   She never uses any of that crap. She doesn't need a
            thing...I think we should sell the house.

EDWARD   What?

MICHAEL   I said, I think we should sell the house.

EDWARD   Who to?

MICHAEL   What kind of stupid question is that? I don't know
            who to. That's why you sell them, so you can find out.

EDWARD   I thought you wanted it.

MICHAEL   I don't want the friggin' house.

EDWARD   You don't?

MICHAEL   No. You want it?

EDWARD   I live fifteen hundred miles away, I don't live here.
            You do.

MICHAEL   No, I don't really.

EDWARD   Get real—your bedroom's upstairs.

MICHAEL   So's yours.

EDWARD   That's not what I mean, you know what I mean. This is your address. What do you want to do? Go out and live at the camp full time?

MICHAEL   Maybe.

EDWARD   But what if you decide to get married and have a family?

MICHAEL   I'm never gettin' married again.

EDWARD   (*pausing*) Is something wrong with Mom?

        MICHAEL *shrugs.*

EDWARD   She seems great since I've been here.

MICHAEL   Yeah well, she's off my friggin' back for awhile.

EDWARD   About what?

MICHAEL   About what? About you. She's been driving me nuts. (*mimics*) "Should we put him in his old bedroom or in the spare room? Does he hate fish? Do you hate fish? Who hates fish? Would he eat some mackerel if I bought some mackerel?" She wanted me to bring in a ladder from the garage so she could paint your ceiling.

EDWARD   Aw.

MICHAEL   Aw? Aw shit. She can't go climbing friggin' ladders, she's too damn old. Last month I caught her standing on top of the fireplace, trying to knock down a cobweb with a wooden spoon.

EDWARD   Jesus, she could hurt herself.

MICHAEL   Hurt herself? Christ, she could kill herself...and she's having spells.

EDWARD   What kind of spells?

MICHAEL   I don't know. All I know is I come home from work one day and find her stretched out on the living room floor, snoring away. She says she got tired cause she was rearranging the furniture, so she lay down and had a "little nap." Told me the hardwood floor was good for her back.

EDWARD   Was she okay afterwards?

MICHAEL   She says she's fine, gets mad if I even mention it...but here last week a couple of Al LeBlanc's kids found her lying on the beach at the foot of Murphy Street. Eight o'clock in the morning. They got Al from the garage and he drove her home. I didn't even know about it till last night when I took her car down to have the oil changed and Al asked me how she was.

EDWARD   God. When was the last time she saw her doctor?

MICHAEL   Dr. Quack?

EDWARD   She still seeing that jerk?

MICHAEL   (*imitating* EMMA) "He was a friend of your father's." It wasn't long ago she had her big check-up. Couple of weeks ago. She said everything was fine, but...

EDWARD   But he's a moron.

MICHAEL   You got it. (*pausing*) Everything's changed now since Dad died. Everything.

EDWARD   Sell the house. Jesus. She was born here, up in my old room...what do you think we should do?

MICHAEL   How the hell should I know? You're the smart one.

They sit a moment. Black.

Early morning at the beach. EMMA *has been walking along the shore. She has just put the flashlight into her shopping bag.*

The porch, a few minutes later. The sound of crows. EDWARD *steps outside to look for his mother just as she returns from her walk.*

EMMA   Good morning.

EDWARD   Good morning, where have you been?

EMMA   I couldn't sleep so I went out for a little walk.

EDWARD   Where?

EMMA   Down along the shore.

EDWARD   All by yourself?

EMMA   Yes. Why, you think I've got a man stashed away down there?

EDWARD   What if something happened?

EMMA   What could happen?

EDWARD   Anything?

EMMA   Safest time to be down there. All the hoodlums and their dune buggies are asleep.

EDWARD   You can't go off without anyone knowing where you are.

EMMA   My Maker knew where I was.

EDWARD   Oh great. And he can dial 911 if you slip and fall.

EMMA   What makes you think I'm gonna slip and fall? I'm
            not that old and frail yet, Boy!

EDWARD   I didn't say you were, I just...

EMMA   I could just as easily slip and fall here in the house if
            that's what you're worried about, and where would
            that leave me most of the time? You off in the big city
            and your brother off at work or out at that camp of
            his...What makes you so sure I'll slip and fall?

EDWARD   I never said I was sure. I just said maybe you
            shouldn't go off without letting someone know where
            you are.

EMMA   You'll appreciate it when you get back to your
            precious *Trono* and I phone you up at five A.M. and
            say, "Eddie dear, I'm going for a walk now."

EDWARD   Now you're being silly.

EMMA   You're the one who's being silly. Next thing you
            know, you'll be trying to move me into some old
            home. Lock me away.

EDWARD   Jeeze, what's your problem today?

EMMA   I don't have a problem. (*pausing*) When I was coming
            up from the shore just now there was an ambulance in
            front of Vyia Rodd's place. They were putting her in
            the back just as I got there.

EDWARD   The old witch sick?

EMMA   Not any more. One of her neighbours saw the TV light
                 on about an hour ago—Melody Quaid, you know her?
                 So she went over and looked in the window. Vyia was
                 sittin' there dead in front of the TV.

EDWARD   Vyia Rodd is dead?

EMMA   Poor old thing.

EDWARD   Poor old thing!

EMMA   Now, Ed, none of us are perfect.

EDWARD   Mom, I can't believe you!

EMMA   She's had a terrible winter. And she did work darn
                 hard for that little church. She organized the Lobster
                 Suppers for a good twenty-five years.

EDWARD   Yes, and you bitched about the way she did it every
                 time, so don't start feeling sorry for Vyia Rodd just
                 because she's dead. She treated you and Dad like dirt
                 and she was terrible to Michael. She used to lock him
                 in the janitor's cupboard if he didn't get his work right.

EMMA   I didn't know that.

EDWARD   Yes, you did. You did because I came home and told
                 Dad and he didn't do a damn thing about it. Not a
                 thing.

EMMA   And what could he have done? You couldn't do a
                 damn thing around here anyway.

EDWARD   He could have tried.

EMMA   And then she would have picked on the kid even
                 more. Or maybe she would have started picking on
                 you too. And the whole mess would have spilled over

EMMA   into the Church where she was in cahoots with that
            darned Reverend "Bob" cause she thought he might
            be stupid enough to marry her. That's the way
            everything always works around here, you know that.

EDWARD   Oh, you guys drive me nuts.

EMMA   Well, I'm sorry some of us aren't perfect!

            EMMA *exits into the house.* EDWARD *moves
            towards the beach.*

> EDWARD *is standing on the beach. The weather is grey although the sun is trying to break through the clouds.*

PAT   (*off*) Yowsa yowsa yowsa!

> EDWARD *turns quickly and looks up the beach.* PAT *runs to him.*

PAT   Surprise surprise!

EDWARD   Pat! Hi baby!

> *They embrace each other.* EDWARD *spins her around.*

PAT   I thought it was you down here. God, what's happened to you? You're so trim.

EDWARD   I've been lifting weights.

PAT   You? What brought this on?

EDWARD   Turning thirty-eight.

PAT   So you've been at it for quite awhile then.

EDWARD   Aren't you cute? Dying your hair?

PAT   Thanks for being so subtle, I'm practically grey. Aren't we pathetic?

EDWARD   You're down here early.

PAT   Yep.

EDWARD   Is everything all right in Rexton?

PAT   Rexton is Rexton. Mom and Aunt Horna complain as much as ever, but they're okay. How's your Mom?

EDWARD   She seems fine but, you know, who can tell? She's stubborn as usual. And Mike's Mike.

PAT   Oh...He's around? Am I stupid to be here?

EDWARD   We're all stupid to be here. Am I ever glad to see you!

PAT   Yeah.

EDWARD   How's everything?

PAT   A lot better now that I've escaped from Mom and Aunt Horna I can tell ya. Their latest is ceramics—you know lobster ashtrays, skunk salt and peppers.

EDWARD   Oh, God, this place drives me mental!

PAT   I suppose you'd rather be in Toronto right now.

EDWARD   You bet.

PAT   Oh great. First time we're here together in fifteen years and you'd rather be someplace where people are dropping dead from the humidity.

EDWARD   Well, I miss it.

PAT   Why? You in love or something?

EDWARD   No.

PAT   Oh, I see. (*pausing*) Does he know it?

EDWARD   What's that supposed to mean?

PAT   Oh, he doesn't love you back.

EDWARD   Is that supposed to be a joke?

PAT   God, you're touchy.

EDWARD   Sorry.

PAT   Yeah, well, maybe I'm not very funny anymore these days.

EDWARD   Something's the matter?

PAT   I came home early because I've given Mark a week to get out of the house. He was having another affair with one of his students.

EDWARD   Another?

PAT   I think. His sister found out and told me about it last week. Poor Jean—she's one of my best friends. Anyway, that's it, kaput, c'est ca.

EDWARD   I've always known he was a jerk.

PAT   If I wanted I-told-you-so's I could have stayed with Mom in Rexton. And you've never even met him.

EDWARD   I didn't have to meet the bonehead.

PAT   If you'd come to visit me once in the last five years, you could have based your opinion on personal experience.

EDWARD   I'm sorry I went to New York instead of Edmonton that time. I got confused.

PAT   I'll say you got confused. And please, spare me your little speech about hick towns where people go body

PAT   surfing in shopping malls, I like it there just fine.
               Except for Mark.

EDWARD   I'm sorry Patty. I know how much you loved him.

               EDWARD *hugs her.*

PAT   Oh, Eddie, I'm such a sucker for weak men. They
               always tell you what you want to hear because that
               way you won't hate them. I think it's because they're
               so romantic.

EDWARD   What?

PAT   Don't you think weak men are romantic? They always
               get you to eat strawberries with them in the bathtub or
               something. By candlelight.

EDWARD   So he's moving out.

PAT   And she's helping him—isn't that sweet? I met her,
               you know. Mark had a couple of his students over for
               dinner one night. She helped me load the dishwasher.
               This is before, you know, before I found out. I think
               he enjoyed the guilt. She's really young. I mean real
               young.

EDWARD   Well, I'm glad you've finally seen the light.

PAT   You do the same thing. You stuck with that Floyd idiot
               for over two years.

EDWARD   Let's leave Floyd out of this.

PAT   How could you even like someone with a name like
               that? Flo-y-yd—God you just say it and you sound
               like you're whining. And Mark was at least educated.

EDWARD   He was just a jock with a degree.

PAT   Three degrees.

EDWARD   Who cares how many? He could win the Nobel Prize and he'd still be a jerk.

PAT   He was real smart. (*sighing*) And real good lookin'.

      MICHAEL *and* DAVID *enter behind* PAT.

EDWARD   You.

DAVID   Yeah, me.

PAT   (*turning*) Michael! Hello.

MICHAEL   Patricia.

      They stand frozen a moment. Then PAT *goes to* MICHAEL. *Kisses him.*

PAT   How are you? You look taller.

MLKE   I'm the same.

PAT   (*to* DAVID) Hi. I'm Pat.

EDWARD   Sorry. Pat this is David. David, this is my friend Pat.

      DAVID *and* PAT *shake hands.*

PAT   Hi.

DAVID   Hi. (*pausing*) You're Pat from Edmonton!

PAT   I guess so. Yes.

DAVID   This is terrific. I hear about you all the time.

PAT   (*looking at* MICHAEL) Oh?

DAVID   Yeah, he talks about you every day.

PAT   (*to* MICHAEL) You do?

EDWARD   No. I do.

PAT   Sorry. I thought you were a friend of Michael's.

DAVID   No, we just met.

PAT   Oh.

EDWARD   David's from Toronto.

PAT   Ah.

DAVID   Yeah. I just got into town a few minutes ago. Michael
             was the only one home and he drove me here.

PAT   You just arrived from Toronto.

DAVID   Yes.

PAT   Oh.

EDWARD   And how'd you get here?

DAVID   Car. There was an ad for a ride to Halifax in NOW
             Magazine.

EDWARD   Oh.

DAVID   Just a spur of the moment thing you know, just...

PAT   That's great. (*pausing, then to* MICHAEL) How's
             everything going?

MICHAEL   The same.

PAT   Anything new?

MICHAEL   No. (*pausing*) Vyia Rodd died.

PAT   Huh?

MICHAEL &   (*simultaneously*) My old teacher.
EDWARD   Our old teacher.

MICHAEL   (*pausing*) She died. Finally.

PAT   She the one who locked you in the closet?

DAVID   What?

EDWARD   We didn't get to go to alternative schools.

DAVID   Yeah, but—

MICHAEL   It's gonna rain soon. Is that your car up there? I'm
               over this way.

PAT   Yeah, that's mine, my brother's. Who wants a lift with
               who?

EDWARD   Well...

DAVID   (*to* EDWARD) Can we walk back? I've been in a car
               all night. It's not very far.

EDWARD   Um, sure. Why don't you two go on ahead. We'll be
               up at the house in a few minutes.

MICHAEL   See ya (*exiting quickly*)

DAVID   Thanks, Michael.

PAT   You'll probably get wet.

EDWARD   We won't be that long.

PAT   Please, because Mike and me...you know.

EDWARD   I know. We'll walk up and be right there. Go on ahead
             and say hi to Mom.

DAVID   We just drove by your Mom. Mike said she was
             coming back from the post office.

EDWARD   So she hasn't seen you yet.

DAVID   No.

PAT   Are you sure I can't give you a lift?

EDWARD   We'll be right there.

PAT   Okay. See you soon. (*exiting*) But you're gonna get
             soaked!

             EDWARD *and* DAVID *both look after* PAT.
             An awkward moment.

DAVID   It's beautiful here.

EDWARD   Yeah?

DAVID   (*pausing*) So hi.

             EDWARD *looks out at the water.* DAVID
             *looks at him. A pause and they they both
             speak at the same time.*

EDWARD   What—

DAVID   I—

EDWARD   Sorry.

DAVID   Go ahead.

EDWARD   No you.

DAVID   It was nothing.

EDWARD   Oh?

DAVID   I just...I finished the calendar. You know, those drawings I was doing for that real estate guy.

EDWARD   Oh.

DAVID   Yeah.

EDWARD   How'd it go?

DAVID   Alright. They like it—it's what they wanted. It's boring.

EDWARD   You're good at that stuff.

DAVID   Must be my mother's influence, huh? It was like being forced to design her dream home over and over again.

EDWARD   (*pausing*) And you drove down with some people from Halifax.

DAVID   Yeah. Two straight guys who played Twisted Sister all night. It was pretty awful. (*pausing*) This is a real problem for you, isn't it?

EDWARD   I've been trying to phone you for a week.

DAVID   It's been so hot there that I've been staying over at Ava's place on Ward's Island. (*pausing*) Breeze off the

DAVID	lake at night, you know, easier to work. Oh, and I gave her the chair, the Fifties chair.
EDWARD	The answering machine hasn't even been on.
DAVID	I know. I'm a little prick?

DAVID *touches* EDWARD, *who moves away a bit.*

EDWARD	You didn't have to get rid of the chair.
DAVID	Yes, I did. She and I took it across on the ferry the night before last.
EDWARD	Look, David, the chair wasn't the problem.
DAVID	Come on, you called it furniture from Hell.
EDWARD	They're only the Fabulous Fifties to people who didn't have to live through them. Why didn't you even answer the phone?
DAVID	Cause I didn't want to talk to you.
EDWARD	So what the hell are you doing here?
DAVID	Apologizing in the flesh.
EDWARD	That's just dandy.
DAVID	I wanted to see you.
EDWARD	Look, babe, the last time you saw me, you couldn't get out of my place fast enough. Our big lobster dinner and the water wasn't even boiling when suddenly you're telling me I'm a total fraud and dinner is off. You slammed the door. And here it is,

EDWARD	what, seven days later and fifteen hundred miles away, and you come strolling up to me on the beach.
DAVID	I was really mad at you.
EDWARD	(*pausing*) Why didn't you call me first?
DAVID	Because I didn't want you to get all weird about your family and talk me out of it. Toronto's unbearable right now and I missed you. I even went out the other night to the Rock and Roll Fag bar, you know, and...
EDWARD	And what?
DAVID	And nothing, what do you think? I just, you know, I've just been horny and I missed you and I'm sorry we had a fight and...you wish I hadn't come.
EDWARD	I didn't say that. I didn't say that at all. But why didn't you just call me and tell me you wanted to come here?
DAVID	Aren't you even glad to see me?
EDWARD	(*pausing*) Yes, of course I'm glad to see you. I just don't know what to do.
DAVLD	We can neck.
EDWARD	I mean...
DAVID	We can neck, we can go swimming. I can meet your mother.

Thunder sounds.

EDWARD	(*looking at the dark sky*) Oh, great.

DAVlD *kisses* ED.

DAVID   (*looking at the sky*) Yikes.

EDWARD   Yikes.

They both run off to avoid the rain.

At the house. EMMA *sees* PAT *running up the steps.*

EMMA   Patsy!

PAT   Hi!

They embrace.

EMMA   My goodness, what a surprise!

PAT   Didn't Ed tell you I called?

EMMA   Yes, I just wasn't expecting to see you so soon.

PAT   I just escaped from my mother's.

EMMA   Oh dear.

PAT   Mom, you look great.

EMMA   Oh, what an old fibber you are. I must look like something from the Fiji Islands. But you've gained a little weight. Looks good on you.

PAT   Just two or three pounds.

EMMA   Makes all the difference. After we saw you that night last summer, Mac said he thought you looked too thin.

PAT   Yeah? That was a nice dinner.

EMMA   Yes, that's a nice little restaurant up there in Buctouche, isn't it? You see, there can be decent places to eat in the poor old Maritimes.

MICHAEL *arrives.*

MICHAEL	Don't start with the poor old Maritimes, Christ.
EMMA	Mike, look who's here.
MICHAEL	I know, I know, I saw her down at the beach with Ed.
EMMA	Oh, where's he then? You didn't leave him down there in that cloudburst.
MICHAEL	He wanted to walk.
PAT	He's walking back with his friend from Toronto.
EMMA	Which friend? Who's that?
PAT	David. He just got here a little while ago.
EMMA	(*to* MICHAEL) Oh, was that who you had in your car?
MICHAEL	Umhum.
EMMA	Is he staying here?
MICHAEL	How the hell should I know?
EMMA	There's always room for one more, I suppose. You'll be staying for a couple of days, won't you Patsy?
PAT	I'd love to if there's room.
EMMA	Oh, someone can always sleep in the attic. Ed loves it up there.
PAT	Great. Oh, Mike, Arnie said to tell you that the electrical generator is still up for grabs if you want it. He said you'd know what it was all about.

MICHAEL   Yeah.

EMMA   Now, what would that be for?

MICHAEL   What do you think it would be for?

EMMA   That's why I asked, I'm stupid, I don't know.

PAT   It's for your camp, isn't it?

>   MICHAEL *nods.*

EMMA   See? Now, I know. So, Patsy, how's your family?

PAT   Oh, good. Linda had a baby, another girl. Arnie's getting married in the fall. Although her family says she's too good for him—and, of course, she and mother don't get along.

EMMA   And how are you and your mother doing these days?

PAT   Oh, okay. But I'm sure glad I'm living in Edmonton.

EMMA   That's too bad. Oh, you can tell me something. Are there really submarines in the Mall out there?

PAT   That's what I hear.

EMMA   You mean to say you've never been?

PAT   Nope, never have.

EMMA   And you right handy, too. There's people from here who travel out there just to see it.

PAT   And there's people who come from all over just for the Lobster Carnival. You going this year?

EMMA   You won't catch me anywhere near that darn old
            thing. It's just a tourist trap. (*to* MICHAEL) Is this
            fellow the same David that Ed's been trying to phone
            all week?

MICHAEL   How the hell should I know?

EMMA   You met him, didn't you?

MICHAEL   Sorry, but I forgot to ask him if Ed had been trying to
            phone him.

EMMA   Don't get smart, you know what I mean.

PAT   Did Ed say this was his boyfriend?

EMMA   Oh, I wouldn't know.

MICHAEL   This David guy?

PAT   Yeah.

MICHAEL   What happened to Floyd?

PAT   That ended five years ago, thank God. Just after I
            moved to Edmonton.

EMMA   You're going to think I'm terrible, but I didn't care for
            him. He was, well, do you know what I mean when I
            say "sleazy?" That Floyd was sleazy. He was always
            acting, always putting it on. Now, I can't say that he
            wasn't nice to me. He was just...

PAT   I'd say sleazy pretty well covers it.

EMMA   Whatever. It's none of my business.

PAT   Did you like him, Mike?

MICHAEL	He was okay. Talked too much. You want a beer?
PAT	Oh, yes, thanks.
MICHAEL	You want something? Rum?
EMMA	It's the afternoon still!
PAT	Oh, come on, Mom, live a little.
EMMA	Well, alright. Just this once. A little rum'd be nice. Very little. With some Diet Coke, thank you kindly.

        MICHAEL *exits.*

EMMA	What do you know about this David?
PAT	Nothing at all, I just met him. He seems nice. He's young.
EMMA	How young?
PAT	I don't know—twenties.
EMMA	I won't know what to say to him.
PAT	Try, "I'm very pleased to make your acquaintance."
EMMA	That's not what I mean.
PAT	You'll be fine—he won't bite…Mike seems good.
EMMA	He's doing very well at the office, I understand.
PAT	That's great. Oh, it's so good to see you.
EMMA	I'm glad to see you, too. You know, I think quite often about that time you phoned me. It was really good of you to take the trouble.

PAT   Oh, Mom, it was the least I could do. You and Mac have been really good to me.

EMMA He did think you were pretty special.

PAT   Well, I thought he was, too. He always laughed at my bad jokes.

EMMA If there was anyone on earth capable of helping Ed and his father see eye to eye on things, it was you.

PAT   Yeah, well—both pretty stubborn guys.

EMMA Oh, I guess we all are down here—bad trait sometimes. You must be relieved to be with a fella from the West. I'm so glad that's working out for you, dear, I'm glad you're settled down.

PAT   Yeah.

EMMA But tell me—are things any easier with you and your mother this time?

PAT   Well, no, not really. It's not terrible, but…I do understand more about how hard it must have been for her with my father drinking like he did. But, well, when I come home it's really to see Arnie and my sisters and their kids.

EMMA Some of those kids must be teenagers by now.

PAT   Don't remind me, Mom, please. I feel so old when I think about it.

EMMA You old—ha. You're still a spring chicken yet. (*pausing*) You know, I hope that seeing you might do Mike some good.

PAT   Oh, well, yes, I hope so too.

EMMA   I know that things didn't work out for you two back
            then, but, well, he has a tendency to hide, you know,
            to hide out from things. I think just seeing you a little
            might do him some good. He's been down in the
            dumps lately. I think he misses his father.

PAT   Yeah, I suppose. Well, we all do.

EMMA   I'd never seen Mac laugh so hard as he did sometimes
            those summers when you used to come visit. One
            night he got in bed with me and he took into
            laughing—he laughed and laughed. I thought he'd
            never get to sleep.

PAT   Why?

EMMA   Oh, it was that night we got carrying on and we were
            dancing and acting the fool. (*laughing*) When you dug
            out those old hats of mine and put them on everyone's
            heads—I can see Mac and the boys yet. They looked
            so darn funny. Poor old Mac laughed half the night.
            And we were so tired the next day cause we got up
            real early for something. To pack a lunch for you kids,
            I think.

PAT   We were going camping.

EMMA   Right. You and the boys were going to P.E.I. camping.

PAT   Yeah.

EMMA   And you came home engaged.

PAT   Yes. Yes we did.

            Quiet. MICHAEL *returns with beer for
            himself and* PAT, *rum for* EMMA.

PAT   Thanks, Michael.

EMMA   Thank you kindly, sir.

             Pause.

EMMA   Funeral's going to be tomorrow. They're not wasting
             any time.

MICHAEL   Good.

PAT   This that old witch who locked you in the closet?

EMMA   Everyone seems to know about that closet but me.

             EDWARD *enters with* DAVID, *both wet from
             the rain.*

EDWARD   Just started pouring buckets. Hi everybody. Mom, this
             is David, my friend from Toronto. David, this is my
             mother, Emma.

EMMA   (*extending her hand*) I'm very pleased to make your
             acquaintance.

DAVID   (*shaking her hand*) Hi. I hope it's alright, me arriving
             like this.

EMMA   No, no, we don't stand on formality here.

             MICHAEL *takes his beer and exits quietly.*

EDWARD   David was lucky enough to get a ride right to town.

EMMA   Really.

DAVID   Edward talks about home so much that when I had the
             chance to come down here, I just went for it.

EMMA   Oh.

DAVID   I've never been east of Montreal before.

EMMA   Well, we'll have to show you the sights, won't we?

EDWARD   Yeah. We can all go into Moncton, wait for the Tidal Bore.

EMMA   Oh, Ed, it's not all that bad around here. But look at you, you're wet. You two should go and change before you catch cold.

EDWARD   Come on. I'll show you my room.

DAVID   This is a great house.

EMMA   It suits me.

EDWARD   Come on.

                EDWARD *and* DAVID *exit.*

EMMA   I should go dig out some clean sheets for you kids. I'll put you in the spare room. Should I put the boys in the same bed?

PAT   (*shrugging*) You okay, Mom?

EMMA   Yes, yes. I'm fine, fine.

                PAT *smiles.* EMMA *exits.* PAT *sips her drink.*

                MICHAEL *is outside watching* PAT *through the window. He drinks his beer and stands in the yard watching her.*

That evening after dinner. EMMA *and* PAT
are looking at a photo album.

PAT   Mac was good looking wasn't he?

EMMA   Well, I always thought so. Ed looks like him, don't
you think?

PAT   Umhum.

EMMA   They didn't agree about much, those two, but they
sure agreed about you.

     EDWARD *enters.*

EDWARD   Who?

EMMA   You and your father.

EDWARD   Oh.

PAT   Is David having a nap?

EDWARD   He's lying down, he's exhausted.

EMMA   That's a long drive from Toronto straight through.

PAT   Was Mac the only man you ever went out with?

EMMA   No, no. Go back a couple of pages. There. No, one
more. There. See that fellow standing next to Ed's
Aunt Jane?

PAT   You went out with him! Yowsa, Mom, he's a
knock-out. Ed, check this guy out.

EDWARD   (*looking at album*) Who is it?

EMMA   Fellow by the name of Billy Hat.

EDWARD   Yeah? Who was he?

EMMA   He lived up country near my grandmother's farm. I used to go and visit his sister Kitty.

EDWARD   I've never heard of him before.

EMMA   There's lots of things you've never heard of. You don't know everything you know.

PAT   When did you meet Dad?

EMMA   Oh, we never met. We always knew each other.

PAT   Really?

EMMA   There was a gang of us who used to chum around together and he kind of hung around with us. He was so darn quiet I didn't pay any attention to him for years.

PAT   What happened?

EMMA   Nothing happened. Things just changed, that's all. Things got different...Here one night near the end of summer I was walking along the shore. I'd just had a big fight with my sister Jane and I was real ugly. I was sailing right along when I ran into poor old Mac down there lugging rocks for that damn rock garden of his mother's. Every year she got him to rebuild the damn thing and every blessed year it got washed away in a fall storm. And she couldn't even grow a weed that looked like anything. It was late at night and the poor fella was down there slaving away in the dark. And I thought, I've got it darn easy. What would I be like if I

EMMA   had a miserable family like his? And by the time the
              next summer rolled around, I did. The whole shebang!

PAT   Ha.

EDWARD   What happened to Billy Hat?

EMMA   He moved to the Boston States.

EDWARD   Did he marry?

EMMA   No, he died a bachelor here about five years ago.

EDWARD   Yeah? (*looking at photo again*)

PAT   Oh, get that look off your face.

EDWARD   What look?

PAT   You think everybody who doesn't get married is gay.

EDWARD   I do not.

EMMA   Billy Hat?

EDWARD   It's not impossible.

EMMA   Billy Hat did not have the same problem you do.

EDWARD   Do we have to call it a "problem?"

PAT   Well it hasn't always been a solution.

EMMA   Oh, Eddie, you know I don't mean to sound narrow
              minded. And I can't say "gay." It reminds me of Vyia
              Rodd. One sip of wine and she threw herself at
              anything in pants. (*imitating*) "Oh, I feel so gay all of
              a sudden, just so giddy and gay." Any other word is
              fine.

EDWARD   Well "problem" isn't.

PAT   When did you fall in love with Mac?

EMMA   Oh, I don't know. I just knew I was.

PAT   Come on, Mom. You make it sound like it wasn't romantic at all.

EMMA   I never said that.

EDWARD   Was Dad capable of a romantic gesture?

EMMA   You have no idea what your father was capable of.

EDWARD   No?

PAT   So you can't remember when you fell in love?

EMMA   You know something? I don't understand all this business about falling in love. I can be as big a romantic fool as the next person, but falling in love? Na.

EDWARD   What do you mean?

EMMA   I mean the difference between falling in love and being in love. Falling in love is kidstuff. It's just a crush. Like you—that time you had that big crush on Hop Hebert.

PAT   Hop Hebert?

EDWARD   I was just a kid.

EMMA   And you thought he walked on water. It was "Hop did this" and "Hop did that." Hop Hop Hop the whole summer. You drove you father and me crazy. Isn't that right?

EDWARD   So what? I was seven or eight years old.

EMMA   And he was nothing but a common hoodlum.

EDWARD   What are you getting at?

EMMA   Not a thing. I'm just saying that's what a crush is—it's not love. When you grow up, you stop "falling" in love. Am I right?

EDWARD   Are you comparing the feelings I have now to the ones I had when I was a kid?

EMMA   You have to admit, poor Hop wasn't much.

EDWARD   Oh, and neither's David—is that what you're saying?

PAT   Ed.

EMMA   What?

EDWARD   You're as bad as Dad was—always dragging up stupid stuff I did when I was a kid to try and prove I still can't do anything right.

EMMA   And now you know it wasn't all your poor father! It takes two.

EDWARD   My poor father!

PAT   Come on, Ed.

EDWARD   It is all because of David—that's the reason.

EMMA   David?

EDWARD   Yes, David. What are you trying to say?

EMMA   About David? Not a blessed thing.

EDWARD   You are so. You haven't brought up Hop Hebert for years.

EMMA   That's because you usually bring him up—not me. What's poor Hop got to do with David?

EDWARD   That's what I'd like to know.

PAT   Ed, cool your jets.

EDWARD   If you don't want him here, just say so. We can go to the Hotel.

EMMA   Why would I say a thing like that? What you do is none of my business.

EDWARD   Oh, stop saying it's none of your business. If Mike had been going with someone for over a year you'd make it your business. God, he went to a Dolly Parton concert once with some dame from the office and you talked to me about it for two years—practically had him engaged.

PAT   How long have you been with David?

EDWARD   Last July.

PAT   How come you haven't talked to me about him?

EDWARD   Because I usually tell you the day after I meet someone and by the time I've spent a hundred bucks in long distance calls, it's all over.

PAT   Sorry to waste your time!

EDWARD   That's not what I mean.

EMMA   You don't seem to understand the difference between being nosey and being concerned. I don't pry.

PAT   Last July!

EDWARD   Yeah. He brought his work into the gallery.

PAT   So you're going to give the kid a break, give him a
             little show.

EDWARD   No! No, not yet. At this point his technique can't
             support his ideas. But he's got so much talent he
             doesn't know what to do with it all. Wait'll you see his
             work. It knocked me over.

PAT   I bet.

EDWARD   Look. People bring me their stuff all the
             time—everything from paint-by-numbers to turds on a
             stick—and it's not very often that I see someone who
             has so much talent, and who works so hard, and who
             has so much passion for his work when he's still so ...

PAT   Young.

EDWARD   I know he's young. And his work is remarkable.

PAT   And, no doubt, a fabulous kisser to boot.

EDWARD   Yes. But it's his work that thrills me.

PAT   Oh, Ed, come on. I've seen his hair. I've seen his
             mouth.

EDWARD   Yes, he does have a wonderful mouth and—

EMMA   (*standing up*) I'm going to make some tea.

EDWARD   Right. Passion's just something for Frenchmen to do
             in the dark!

PAT   Ed!

EMMA   I don't need to have a stranger's mouth described to
              me, thank you very much.

              MICHAEL *enters.*

MICHAEL   Can't find it anywhere.

EMMA   What?

MICHAEL   The crib board Dad made.

EDWARD   Screw the crib board.

MICHAEL   You're friggin' friendly all of a sudden.

EMMA   Just ignore him, Michael. Go look in my closet in that
              old overnight case of your father's. I think he took
              that crib board to the hospital with him last time.

              MICHAEL *exits.*

EMMA   I'll be making the tea.

              EMMA *exits.*

EDWARD   Great. Now she'll hate him.

PAT   Cool down, will ya? As long as David isn't a jerk
              she'll like him.

EDWARD   What makes you say he's a jerk?

PAT   I didn't say he was a jerk.

EDWARD   Then why say jerk?

PAT   Why say jerk? History. History is why say jerk.
              Historically speaking, you put us in a room with a

PAT   hundred available men and we'll both make a beeline for the biggest jerk.

EDWARD   Oh?

PAT   Come on, look at our men, Eddie. Just line them up and look at them, and what have you got? One wimp after another. And your poor mother met a couple of yours. Look at Todd telling her he'd like to paint her aura.

EDWARD   That was a very long time ago.

PAT   Or Floyd asking her what kind of wine she preferred with fettucini. Pretentious fart box. I wanted to brain him with that damn clay wine cooler of his.

EDWARD   No more about Floyd, okay?

PAT   You going to start standing up for Mr. Insincerity all of a sudden?

EDWARD   I don't want to talk about Floyd anymore.

PAT   Since when did you stop trashing Floyd?

EDWARD   (*pausing*) Since I found out he was sick.

PAT   (*pausing*) Oh.

EDWARD   I talked to his brother last month. He's not doing very well at all. Not at all.

PAT   Oh, God. Doesn't that scare you?

EDWARD   Yes. But everybody I know is scared ... And it was five years ago and hardly the sexual affair of the century—as you no doubt remember.

PAT   Oh, Ed, I'm sorry...Does David know?

EDWARD   Yes. Of course.

PAT   Oh, Ed. (*pausing*) How awful. I never could stand
               Floyd, but this is just so awful.

EDWARD   Yeah, well, and unfortunately it's a way of life now. I
               don't want Mom to know anything about it, okay?

PAT   Yeah, sure.

EDWARD   She'd just worry needlessly.

               DAVID *enters.*

EDWARD   Hi.

DAVID   Hi there.

PAT   Hi.

               DAVID *puts his arm around* EDWARD *and
               gives him an affectionate hug.*

DAVID   Michael says he'll teach me how to play crib.

PAT   You can't play?

DAVID   No, I'm terrible at card games.

PAT   Good. The kind of opponent I like.

EDWARD   So you didn't sleep?

DAVID   No, but I don't really feel tired anymore. I still feel
               like I'm moving though. I can still feel that car.

EDWARD   Just thank God you can't hear it—Twisted Sister,
             Jesus Murphy. And you thought my Schwarzkopf
             records drove you nuts.

PAT   Did I tell you about Mark and the records?

EDWARD   No.

PAT   Oh, you'll like this one. Mark, that idiot, came back
             from a party with his grad students and told me that
             he'd felt out of touch with them because he didn't
             understand any of their music. Not surprising—this is
             a man who has at least fifty recordings of Schubert's
             "Trout Quintet" and plays you comparison excerpts
             from them all. Anyway, Mr. Excitement goes out and
             spends over two hundred dollars on CDs and tapes.
             And do you know what he bought to put his finger on
             the pulse of the graduating class? Bon Jovi,
             Bananarama, and the complete works of Wham and
             Iron Maiden. Bonehead. (*pausing*) Every man I was
             ever involved with loved chamber music. What do
             you suppose that means?

DAVID   All of them?

PAT   Every last one.

EDWARD   Even Michael?

             MICHAEL *has entered unseen behind them*
             with the crib board.

PAT   Oh, he doesn't count. I wasn't involved with poor
             Michael, I was just married to him. Biggest mistake I
             ever made in my life.

MICHAEL *tries to exit, but he is seen, first by the men, then by* PAT. *A very long, horrible pause.*

EMMA　　　(*bustling in*) Tea is now being served in the dining car.

MICHAEL *throws the crib board to the floor and exits. Black.*

End of Act One

Act Two

The next morning the sun is shining outside the house, an hour before Vyia Rodd's funeral. EDWARD jumps through the door in a bathing suit expecting to find DAVID.

EDWARD   TADA! (*seeing no one*) David? David? (*exiting*)

MICHAEL enters in a two-piece suit looking hot, awkward and uncomfortable. He holds something in his jacket pocket.

MICHAEL   (*quietly, secretly*) David?

EMMA   (*off*) Michael!

MICHAEL takes his hand out of his pocket. He stands behind the door. PAT enters wearing a bathing suit. She is pulling a huge T-shirt over her head.

PAT   (*entering*) Ed?

MICHAEL   Wrong again.

PAT   Oh. You look very nice.

MICHAEL shrugs.

PAT   It's really good of you to go with Mom.

MICHAEL   Well, someone has to make sure Vyia's really dead.

PAT   About last night.

MICHAEL   Forget it.

EDWARD   (*entering*) Where's David? I can't find him anywhere.

PAT   Cool your jets, he's downtown.

EDWARD   All by himself?

PAT   Why, isn't he old enough?

EDWARD   Very funny.

PAT   He wanted to know what he could do to help, so I sent him off to buy pop. I don't think he'll get lost.

EDWARD   I just wanted to show him around.

PAT   The official tour?

EDWARD   Yeah, you know, a sort of My Town and Welcome To It.

PAT   I've been on that tour of yours. There's more points of suffering than the Stations of the Cross.

              EMMA *enters in a simple black dress.*

PAT   Yowsa, yowsa, Mom, you look great.

EMMA   It's a nice dress, isn't it?

PAT   Very chic. Where'd you get it?

EMMA   Oh, somewhere quite glamorous, I can assure you.

EDWARD   Off the rack at Chez Francine downtown.

EMMA   Nobody'd know that if you kept your big mouth
            closed. It's the only decent dress I own these days. I
            wore it to Mac's funeral in the fall.

PAT   You look very smart.

EMMA   I have to wear something smart to be in the same
            league as Bright Eyes here. (*putting her arm around*
            MICHAEL)

MICHAEL   Oh, go away.

EMMA   No, I won't. And your suit looks fine. He was trying to
            tell me it wouldn't fit him anymore.

MICHAEL   I was just trying to get out of going to old Vyia's
            funeral.

EMMA   Now, just hold it. It was your idea to come, not mine.

EDWARD   He just wants to see the part where they toss her in the
            cold, cold ground.

EMMA   Ed!

PAT   (*to* EDWARD) Did you find the cooler?

EDWARD   No, Mom, where's the cooler?

EMMA   It's in the cellar. (*to* MICHAEL) Isn't it?

MICHAEL   How the hell should I know?

EDWARD   Well, I couldn't find it down there.

MICHAEL   Hang on Stupid Face. I know where to look. (*exiting*)

EMMA	(*calling after* MICHAEL) And dig out one of those ice packs from the freezer for them.
MICHAEL	(*off*) Yeah, yeah.

> DAVID *enters with shopping bags—pop, fruit, munchies—and a paper bag from the liquor store.*

DAVID	Morning.
EMMA	Hello.
PAT	You get everything?
DAVID	No problem. Is it ever beautiful out there.
EMMA	We've got you to thank for that—you must've brought all this good weather down with you from Toronto.
DAVID	This is paradise.
PAT	A.K.A. "La capitale mondiale du homard."
DAVID	Mais oui, c'est ca.
EMMA	So what do you think of our little town?
DAVID	It's a lot bigger than I thought.
EDWARD	Bigger!
DAVID	Yeah. Well you made it sound like two streets and a wharf. After all the stories you told me about bootleggers, I was surprised to find a real liquor store.
PAT	Ed forgets it's a town—he prefers to think he was raised in a clearing.

EDWARD   Oh, it's a raging metropolis.

DAVID   There are hundreds of cars downtown.

EMMA   It's that darn old carnival.

DAVID   There's even a traffic helicopter.

EMMA   A what?

DAVID   Traffic helicopter.

                EDWARD *laughs.*

DAVID   What's so funny?

EDWARD   It's a ride.

DAVID   A ride?

EDWARD   Yeah, from the fairgrounds. Bird's eye tour of the
                      fabulous "capitale du homard." Traffic helicopter,
                      cripes.

DAVID   Oh, let's all go!

EDWARD   What?

DAVID   Well, have you ever been in a helicopter? I haven't.

EMMA   They say it's quite expensive for the length of time
                      you're up there.

DAVID   But just think of what you'd see on a day like this!

EMMA   You'd just see this old town.

                MICHAEL *enters with a cooler.*

DAVID   Hi Michael.

MICHAEL   Dave.

PAT   Thanks, Mike. David, let's put that stuff in it right now.

DAVID   Sure thing.

                 PAT *and* DAVID *start putting pop in the
                 cooler.*

EMMA   I suppose I should go dig out that little dark purse of
                 mine.

PAT   (*gesturing to liquor bag*) You want that in here?

DAVID   No, it's bourbon. I bought bourbon and then I couldn't
                 get mint at the Co-op.

EDWARD   That's life here in the big city.

EMMA   You want mint? There's mint growing in the back
                 yard.

DAVID   Yeah? Fabulous. Then we can all have mint julips
                 later.

PAT   Really? I've never had one.

DAVID   One of the rare useful things my father taught me
                 when I was a kid.

PAT   Oh, great! We can play crib tonight with Southern
                 accents.

EMMA   Well, you're welcome to as much of it as you want.
                 Ed's father always had a patch of it out there because
                 he liked it on lamb. I better go find that purse. (*exiting*)

DAVID   (*to* MICHAEL) Could you get some drugs?

               MICHAEL *takes a large baggie of grass from his pocket.*

DAVID   Yoo! How much?

MICHAEL   Oh, nothin.

DAVID   What?

MICHAEL   No, take it.

DAVID   You can't do that.

EDWARD   Is it your homegrown?

MICHAEL   Yeah.

EDWARD   (*to* DAVID) Don't pay him a cent, it's like smoking tarpaper.

PAT   You'd say that about Acapulco Gold. You just don't like it.

DAVID   Right. Pat and I'll just lie around the beach and smoke it all ourselves, won't we?

PAT   You said it, Kiddo. Oh, does anyone know where the tide is right now?

DAVID   I do. The woman at the Liquor Store said it would be high in a couple of hours.

PAT   Perfect.

DAVID   Thanks Michael.

MICHAEL   It's nothin.

DAVID   (*opening baggie and sniffing*) Um, that is the best
              smell.

              EMMA *enters.* EDWARD *hears her and*
              grabs the bag from DAVID'S *hand. He*
              doesn't know where to hide it.

EMMA   Michael?

              EDWARD *shoves the bag of grass down the*
              front of his bathing suit where it makes a
              prominent bulge.

EMMA   Should we walk over to the Church or drive?

              DAVID *and* PAT *exchange a look and try*
              very hard not to laugh out loud.

MICHAEL   Whatever.

EMMA   If I thought there'd be a place to park, I'd rather drive.
              I just hate walking to a funeral. (*looking at*
              EDWARD) Is something wrong?

EDWARD   No, why?

EMMA   Cause you look a little queer all of a sudden. Do you
              feel flushed?

EDWARD   (*folding hands awkwardly over his crotch*) I feel fine.

EMMA   Are you certain? You should get a shirt on.

EDWARD   Did you find your purse?

EMMA   I knew I went looking for something. Gettin' old and
              stupid. (*exiting*)

MICHAEL   Nice play Shakespeare.

PAT   (*laughing, her arm about* DAVID'S *waist*) Ed, you
                   looked like a guilty ten-year-old.

                   EDWARD *takes the baggie out of his trunks,*
                   tosses it to DAVID.

EDWARD   She has enough on her plate without knowing you're
                   all a bunch of drug fiends.

DAVID   And we were going to give her a line of coke for her
                   birthday.

PAT   Guess you'll have to think of something else.

EDWARD   Come on, potheads, let's move out.

                   EDWARD *and* DAVID *take the cooler and*
                   exit.

PAT   Michael, I really was a thoughtless smart ass last night.

MICHAEL   Doesn't matter.

PAT   I am sorry.

MICHAEL   S'okay.

PAT   Come down to the beach after the funeral, okay?

                   MICHAEL *shrugs.*

PAT   Maybe you can even get Mom to come.

EDWARD   (*off*) Pat, come on!

PAT   Okay? See you later.

> PAT *exits after* EDWARD *and* DAVID.
> MICHAEL *watches her. After a pause,*
> MICHAEL *exits after* EMMA.

MICHAEL   Are you ready to go to this friggin' thing or what?

*On the beach in the afternoon—intense
sunlight and the sound of waves.* EDWARD
and DAVID *are lying side by side on a
blanket.* EDWARD *reads a book.*

DAVID   It's perfect here.

EDWARD   It used to be better.

             Pause.

DAVID   I can't see Pat.

EDWARD   She's just been gone half an hour. Probably looking
             for shells.

DAVID   This Mark guy she broke up with—you think she's
             still in love with him?

EDWARD   Probably.

DAVID   That's the pits, huh?

             Pause.

DAVID   You really didn't fool around when you were growing
             up?

EDWARD   No.

DAVID   Not even with girls?

EDWARD   No.

DAVID   And no boy ever?

EDWARD   No.

DAVID   Why not?

EDWARD   I told you—there was no one to fool around with.

DAVID   Lots of sexy French guys in town.

EDWARD   I didn't know any.

DAVID   You didn't even play together?

EDWARD   No.

DAVID   How come?

EDWARD   Because we weren't supposed to. (*pausing*) I mean.
we did until we were about five but then we went to
separate schools and...we weren't supposed to hang
out together.

DAVID   And you let that stop you?

Pause.

DAVID   I used to hang out with this guy, Ricky Ambrose.
Drove my father crazy cause he came from the wrong
side of Gerrard Street. Which is why I really liked
him. That and cause he was so tall for his age.

EDWARD   When was this?

DAVID   Before my father left—Grade Five maybe (*pausing*)
Ricky and I'd go into the woods by the Riverdale Zoo
and play this thing we called the Superman Game.

EDWARD   Yeah?

DAVID   It was always the same—of course. Ricky always had to act surprised every time it happened.

EDWARD   What happened?

DAVID   Oh, stuff…

EDWARD   Like?

DAVID   I thought you wanted to read.

EDWARD   Come on.

DAVID   (*laughing and pausing*) Well. Ricky'd be Superman, and I'd be his best friend, okay? And he'd come flying over to my place—which was this clump of bushes—to tell me that Lois Lane was dead.

EDWARD   Dead?

DAVID   Yeah. He'd say something like, "What am I gonna do, ole buddy, they got my girlfriend." So I'd say. "Oh, Superman, you better come inside." (*touching* EDWARD'S *leg*) So we'd crawl into the bushes and pull down our pants.

EDWARD   And?

DAVID   And what do you think? (*laughing*) But all the time we'd be playing with each other. Ricky'd keep yapping about Lois Lane. Poor ole Lois. "What am I gonna do, ole buddy, even her tits are dead."

EDWARD   (*pausing*) That's it?

DAVID   I didn't say it wasn't a stupid game.

EDWARD   Still sounds better than baseball to me.

DAVID   I can't believe that you knew you were gay when you were a kid and you didn't do anything.

EDWARD   Well, believe it. (*pausing*) I can remember when I realized it. I was up in the attic looking at this art book. Flipping back and forth between these two pictures. This Italian Renaissance "Sleeping Beauty" and this statue of a Greek God, you know, all muscles and curly hair.

DAVID   How old were you?

EDWARD   I don't know. Not very old because the statute had those blank eyes, you know, like Orphan Annie's?—and I pencilled in little eyeballs so he wouldn't look so creepy. Ten or twelve? Anyway, I'm flipping back and forth from the Greek hunk to Sleeping Venus, from the man to the woman, to the man to the woman, and you know what I realized?

DAVID   Sleeping Venus has no penis.

EDWARD   (*laughing*) Well, yeah. And I thought, "Oh, oh, this means I'm a queer now and I'm gonna end up just like Clark Gable."

DAVID   Clark Gable?

EDWARD   Oh, not the real Clark Gable, but the one who lived down on Comeau Street. His real name was Romeo Richard. But he went into Louis Taxi one day and told everyone that people had been telling him he looked like Clark Gable. Well, he didn't, not a bit. He didn't even have big ears. But people just started calling him that, just to tease him and it became his name after a while.

DAVID   And he was gay?

EDWARD   I don't know really. People used to say he was, but I
          don't know if he ever did anything, like sex. He just
          combed his hair funny and never got married. Poor
          old Clark. We used to climb trees and holler stupid
          things at him when he walked under. God, we were
          mean. I used to see him in the library and you know, it
          made me feel horrible if he smiled at me. Like he
          knew something about me that nobody else did. Poor
          guy.

DAVID   What happened to him?

EDWARD   He's probably still around. Probably in the Sacre
          Coeur old folks home.

DAVID   (*looking out into the bay*) I didn't know you could
          really smell the salt. And please don't tell me that it
          used to smell better.

EDWARD   Am I that bad?

DAVID   You know how much you bitched about that Fabulous
          Fifties chair I brought to your place?—you're worse
          than that about everything here.

EDWARD   Really?

DAVID   You're pretty hopeless.

EDWARD   You mean if all else fails I don't have a career with
          New Brunswick tourism?

DAVID   Not a chance.

EDWARD   Quelle dommage! I'll have to go back to Toronto.

DAVID   (*pausing*) Have you thought any more about me
          moving in?

EDWARD   How did I know you were going to say that next?

DAVID   And?

EDWARD   And I still don't think it's a good idea.

DAVID   Even though I practically live there already?

EDWARD   David, I don't want to talk about it.

DAVID   How can the smartest guy I know be so stupid?

EDWARD   What the hell do you want to move in for anyway?

DAVID   Oh, Edward, Jesus. To get out of that crummy little room for starters. In that dump of a house I share where you feel so uncomfortable.

EDWARD   Your roommates keep calling me Sir.

DAVID   They do not. Stop trying to sound like an old queen. Look, I want to live with you, isn't that enough?

EDWARD   Why?

DAVID   Why do you think? You think I just want the studio space?

EDWARD   No!

DAVID   So what's wrong with sharing the same house?

EDWARD   You don't want to be tied down like that.

DAVID   I think you've got your pronouns mixed up.

EDWARD   I just don't think we should live together.

DAVID   Then you shouldn't want to know where I am all the time. Shit, you're frustrating!

EDWARD   See, you wouldn't want to live with me. I'd drive you nuts.

DAVID   You could stop trying to.

EDWARD   Look. I'll be forty before—

DAVID   (*interrupting*) I turn twenty-five. I know. Stop repeating yourself—it's a sign of old age. What are you so afraid of?

EDWARD   I don't know...everything?

DAVID   That's so helpful, Thanks.

EDWARD   (*pausing*) Look. Nothing ever worked out for me. I mean, no lover, ever. I'd given up hoping for it. And...

DAVID   And what? Stuff that happened or didn't happen fifteen years ago's got nothing to do with me.

EDWARD   Look. I just didn't begin the morning I met you, you know. There's a whole pile of crap that comes along with me.

DAVID   We can deal with it. (*pausing*) Do you want me to go back home?

EDWARD   How?

DAVID   Is that a yes or a no?

EDWARD   (*pausing*) I never thought we'd last more than a month, you know, I couldn't believe it. But it's gonna be a year soon. It just seems like last week that you

EDWARD turned up at the gallery…showed me your
      drawings…and…

DAVID   And what?

EDWARD And I'm not ready to get old yet. I still haven't made
      love to anybody when I was sixteen.

DAVID   (*pausing*) Well, you're not going to.

EDWARD I know.

      Pause. Then DAVID *embraces* EDWARD.
      They lie together, holding each other
      passionately. PAT *appears behind them. She*
      is about to call out then she sees them kiss.
      She stands watching them, suddenly very
      lonely, not knowing whether to stay or go.
      Lights fade around her.

PAT   Mom?

At EMMA'S *house, that evening.* EMMA
alone as PAT *enters.*

PAT   Mom? All by yourself? Where's Michael?

EMMA   I don't know. He took off somewhere in his car when
we got back from the funeral. Where are the boys?

PAT   They went for a walk; they're down at the wharf.

EMMA   Oh.

PAT   What's the matter?

EMMA   Oh, that darn old twin, Muriel, comes up to us after
the interment and she says to Mike, she says, "Why
don't you or that attractive brother of yours ever get
married?" Mean old thing. Ed tells me I shouldn't let
it get my goat, but I always do, every time. Oh, Patsy,
I worry so.

PAT   What Mom?

EMMA   Did we bring them up all wrong?

PAT   What do you mean?

EMMA   Well, Edward's problem. I find it all so difficult. And
now with so many of them getting AIDS and God
knows what, well, it's not an easy thing to accept.

PAT   I know, but it's not your fault, Mom.

EMMA   But it's not just Edward. It's everything. It's Michael
too. Mac and I just wanted our boys to be happy, that's
all. But do you know what I think is the truth? No

EMMA   matter what we do, and no matter how hard we try or
                how much we care, we're going to get it wrong. Every
                blessed time, it's going to be wrong.

PAT   Oh. Mom.

EMMA   I've been thinking about my Mac all day long. I used
                to worry about how he would manage on his own. He
                joked, you know, that as soon as I was in my grave
                he'd have to marry Vyia Rodd—because she was
                always bragging up her cooking to men. But I was
                sitting in our old pew today looking at Vyia's casket,
                and I wondered if they were together somewhere and
                looking down at me from a cloud. And suddenly I was
                jealous that darn old Vyia might be closer to Mac then
                me. Then I realized that I was thinking crazy things
                and that heaven is just a pretty story for kids. A bed
                time story to quiet them down. I don't believe in any
                of it anymore.

PAT   Mom.

EMMA   It's just a bedtime story. (*pausing*) I just never
                imagined a time when I wouldn't have him to look
                after. And now I'll never see him again.

PAT   But you did have him.

EMMA   Yes, and what he ever saw in a stupid old woman like
                me I'll never know.

PAT   Mom!

EMMA   It's the God's truth.

PAT   It is not!

EMMA   I'm never satisfied. I complain when no one tells me anything, and then when they do, I complain even more.

PAT   But—

EMMA   I hate it when my kids keep secrets from me, but when they tell me the truth, I hate that too. There's just no satisfying me, there never was. All I can do is stick my nose where it doesn't belong. And now I'm old and sick and feeling sorry for myself—I don't even have any use for the Maker anymore. I'm not even worth knowing. I better just get it over with and pack myself off somewhere.

PAT   Mom, don't talk like this!

EMMA   Oh, Patsy, I feel like something big and miserable could just pull me right out and drag me under.

PAT   It's because you're missing him, Mom; it's because you're missing Dad.

EMMA   I've never felt so sorry for myself. You won't say anything to the boys about this, will you?

PAT   Mom.

EMMA   There are some things you can only talk about with another female. I talked to Mac about most things, but there were some things—even the time we lost that little girl. I could never talk to him about her. Some things you can't say to men.

PAT   I suppose.

EMMA   We gals are made of tougher stuff. I felt this way then, I suppose. When Mac drove me home from the hospital, I was in a terrible state. Somethin' awful.

EMMA	(*pausing*) But then, scarcely a year later, little Ed came along, and that all went so smooth.
EDWARD	(*off*) Hello!

EDWARD *and* DAVID *enter after a moment.*

PAT	Hi.
EDWARD	What are you two up to?
EMMA	How was your walk?
EDWARD	The sunset over the Bay was so beautiful,
EMMA	I've said that for years and you told me I was crazy.
DAVID	While we were walking out on the wharf, the sky and all of the Bay turned copper red. And there was this incredible bird, this big blue heron, just standing there in the water, as still as a statue.
EMMA	He's just outfoxing those little fish for his supper.
DAVID	I couldn't believe it was real after a while, it was so still.
EDWARD	So he waded out and tried to touch it.
DAVID	And I was about three meters away and then it was gone. Flying so low it almost touched the water. And not once did it ever seem to notice we were there. Talk about attitude.
EMMA	There was a time when he steered clear of us because of all the junk in the Bay. Once that stupid Town Council got the sewage cleaned up, the herons came back. They nest in those black spruces over on the Island.

DAVID   Yeah? How many?

EMMA   Mike might know—ask him when he gets back. You
               didn't see him on your travels by any chance?

EDWARD   No. Haven't seen him since before the funeral.

DAVID   Can you imagine what a whole colony of them would
               look like? All standing there? All just standing there
               aloof and not watching you?

EMMA   And with that gorgeous sunset—maybe you should
               paint a picture.

EDWARD   You could call it, "By the Shores of Kitschy Goomy."

PAT   (*sarcastically*) Perhaps he could transcend the obvious.

EMMA   Someone will have to tell me what "kitschy" means
               cause I'm stupid.

DAVID &   (*simultaneously*) Bad taste.
PAT   Corny.

EMMA   Oh, like the pictures I like.

EDWARD   Here we go.

EMMA   Well, I like to know what I'm looking at, I do. Your
               father and I wandered around that gallery of yours
               without a clue half the time.

EDWARD   Who'd like a drink?

PAT   Yes.

DAVID   Is now a good time? Should I make them?

PAT   Yeah, how about these famous mint julips.

DAVID   Emma, would you like one?

EMMA   I'll have whatever's goin'.

DAVID   You'll have to show me where the mint is.

EMMA   Yes, you're right. You'll have a hard time finding it in that overgrown mess out back.

DAVID   Do you have a flashlight?

EMMA   Is there one in that grocery bag over there?

DAVID   Yeah.

EMMA   Well, let's go then.

PAT   Mom, relax, he can get it on his own.

EMMA   No, a cow couldn't find her calf out there. I'll go show him. I need to stretch my legs. Come on, kid, let's go.

EMMA *and* DAVID *exit. Pause.*

EDWARD   He has a great idea for her birthday. We should take her for the helicopter ride.

PAT   Are you out of your goddamn mind?

EDWARD   Huh?

PAT   She doesn't want to fly and you know it.

EDWARD   I think she could really like it.

PAT   And I think you're full of shit.

EDWARD   What's with you?

PAT   Nothing.

EDWARD   Come on, what's the matter?

PAT   How old is he exactly?

EDWARD   Oh. He's in his mid-twenties.

PAT   Twenty-what?

EDWARD   Twenty-three, in October.

PAT   Twenty-three in October!

EDWARD   He's young.

PAT   Young! I've got Beatle albums older than that. When we were in university he was...he was—Christ, he was probably in kindergarten.

EDWARD   You think I've never thought of this?

PAT   Not seriously enough, obviously.

EDWARD   You think it doesn't drive me nuts that he's younger than me?

PAT   You've got a crush on a sexy kid.

EDWARD   I do not! God, what's eating you all of a sudden?

PAT   You goddamn men, that's what. Start to get older and what do you do? Head for the playground to rekindle your youth.

EDWARD   Ho! Hey, let's get something straight here. I am not Mark, and David is not some tootsie-pie student of mine.

PAT   Same diff. You're all alike.

EDWARD   (*touching her*) Pat—

PAT   NO! I don't want you to touch me.

EDWARD   I—

PAT   Mark was kind to me, you know? He was very, very—oh, how can I say that he was kind?

EDWARD   Pat.

PAT   Don't touch me! Oh, I'm so mad! I'm so sick of myself for waiting for that shithead to make a commitment. He told me his favourite poem was "Dover Beach" and I knew I could wait forever. Wait, wait, wait. All I do is goddamn wait! Wait for men to come along and then when they do all they do is keep me waiting. I wish to Christ I'd never met you!

EDWARD   What?

PAT   I was better off before you made me fall in love with all that crap—"Dover Beach" and Matisse and goddamn Elisabeth Schwarzkopf singing those four last frigging songs. Without you I'd have left university and gone back to Rexton. Married some guy and been happy as a clam. By now I'd have kids big enough to ride snowmobiles. My sisters' lives aren't so terrible. They aren't terrible at all. In fact, they look pretty goddamn good after you've just spent five years waiting for a commitment from some clown who won't make one, who will never make one. And after the things I did for him. And nothing you do will make yours last either!

EDWARD   What's that supposed to mean?

PAT   I know you. You used to walk down to the wharf with
               me, remember? Back before little Tootsie Pie even
               knew how to walk. Mr. Poetry, Mr.
               The-Sea-Is-Calm-Tonight,
               The-Moon-Lies-Fair-Upon-The-Coast, Mr.
               Fill-Their-Heads-with-Crap! Sure, you can knock him
               over for a few more months, but you and that kid will
               not last!

EDWARD   You're wrong!

PAT   Ha! Not a chance!

EDWARD   Christ, am I sick of that goddamn defeatist attitude!

PAT   And where'd you think I got that from?

EDWARD   You got it from here, it comes from here! It comes
               from the friggin' fuckin' sandy shores of this goddamn
               neck of the woods! It was bred into us and I'm sick of
               it!

               In the darkness outside, EMMA *and* DAVID
               are walking back from the garden, EMMA'S
               *flashlight illuminating the way. Suddenly the
               light swings and falls.*

EMMA   Oh!

               EMMA *is on the ground.*

DAVID   What's—Edward! Edward!

               In the darkness, DAVID *is bending over*
               EMMA.

DAVID   Emma, are you alright? Emma?

EMMA *moans.*

DAVID   Emma? Jesus. EDWARD? EDWARD?

EDWARD *and* PAT *run out from the house.*

EDWARD   What happened?

DAVID   Help me.

PAT   Oh, no.

PAT *picks up the flashlight and shines it on* EMMA *while* DAVID *and* EDWARD *carry her into the house.*

DAVID   She just went down.

EDWARD   She's passed out.

EMMA   I have not.

PAT   Mom, are you alright?

EMMA   I'm fine.

EDWARD   What happened?

DAVID   She fainted or something.

EMMA   Just let me sit down.

PAT   Maybe she should lie down.

EMMA   A chair is fine.

EDWARD   Pat's right, Mom, you should lie down.

EMMA   Put me in my chair.

                They are inside the house. They help EMMA
                into her chair.

DAVID   We picked the mint. We were talking about her birthday
                and walking back and she just started to go down.

EDWARD   Oh, Christ, she's out again!

EMMA   I am not.

EDWARD   Oh, good, you were under there for a minute.

EMMA   I'm perfectly fine. It's the wine I had with dinner. Old
                Girl's not used to it.

PAT   How do you feel now, Mom?

EMMA   I feel fine. Poor David. I hope I didn't scare you too
                much.

DAVID   Are you feeling better?

EMMA   I was just a little weak, just a weak spell.
                It's nothing.

EDWARD   Nothing!

EMMA   It's nothing to get in a big flap about.

EDWARD   I think I should drive you to Out Patients.

EMMA   I am not driving twenty miles to sit in some waiting
                room till four A.M. so some pipsqueak intern can tell
                me I shouldn't drink so much!

EDWARD   You had one glass of wine.

EMMA   It was big enough for two.

EDWARD   It was not.

EMMA   It was so.

EDWARD   Why are you so goddamn stubborn?

PAT   Why are you arguing with Mom?

EDWARD   She's my mother and I'll argue with her if I want to.

DAVID   Edward.

PAT   Oh, grow up. And you two wanted to send her up in a goddamn helicopter.

EDWARD   What's that got to do with anything?

PAT   She's seventy-five.

EDWARD   She doesn't have to pedal it, she just has to sit in the damn thing!

EMMA   Sit in what?

PAT   Oh, these two clowns thought they'd send you up in that helicopter tomorrow.

EMMA   I know. David was telling me out in the yard. And you know, I think it sounds like it might be kinda fun.

PAT   What?

EDWARD   Maybe Pat's right. You should take it easy for a couple of days.

EMMA   I think that I am perfectly capable of being airborne for ten minutes. And I want all this worrying and arguing to stop. Right now!

Lights fade around EMMA.

An hour later. EDWARD *and* DAVID *are*
talking. DAVID *rolls a joint.*

EDWARD   I can't separate her from this place. I can't. They are
          the same thing. But I hate this place and I love her.
          How do you figure that one?

DAVID   Dunno...Have some of this.

EDWARD   You're not going to smoke that in the house, are you?

DAVID   Ed, she's asleep. Come on, let's have a toot and go to
          bed.

EDWARD   No, I don't want any.

DAVID   What you need.

          While EDWARD *speaks,* DAVID *starts*
          smoking the joint.

EDWARD   Last thing I need (*watching* DAVID) Know something
          stupid? I didn't expect my father to die. Some part of
          you stays a little kid that thinks they'll live forever,
          you know?

DAVID   I guess. My kid sister thought we'd find Grampa at
          the Imperial Six cause he used to take us to the
          movies.

EDWARD   Dad hated the movies.

DAVID   Which is why you like them so much. (*pausing*) My
          father took me golfing—I still think it's the most
          boring activity known to man.

EDWARD   Too bad he didn't take you out to drug dens.

DAVID   God you're an old woman. You'd think I was stoned
          every night of the week. (*pausing*) You and your Dad
          ever do anything together?

EDWARD   Fight. That count?

DAVID   Let's go to bed.

EDWARD   No. I'm not tired.

DAVID   That's why I want to go up now.

EDWARD   You go on up.

DAVID   I want you to come with me.

EDWARD   No, I want to wrap up Mom's present and...

DAVID   (*touching him*) Wrap it tomorrow.

EDWARD   (*moving away*) No, I want to do it now.

DAVID   But—

EDWARD   I need a minute by myself, okay?

DAVID   (*pausing*) You don't want me, do you?

EDWARD   What?

DAVID   Well except for about ten minutes on the beach this
          afternoon—which I instigated—you've barely
          touched me. I want to go to bed, you don't want to
          come. Look, I'm sorry about your mother but keeping
          your hands off me isn't gonna make her live forever.

EDWARD   What are you talking about?

DAVID   Us. I thought if I came here we'd get rid of a whole lot
             of bullshit. I thought, his father died, that's a big
             deal—I was dense enough to think that if you didn't
             have to keep me hidden from that old lady upstairs
             that things might get sensible. I thought she was the
             problem. But it's not her, it's you. You want to be
             alone so you can be a nice boy for Mom and Dad. But
             Dad's dead and she could live with it, if you'd let her.

EDWARD   That's—

DAVID   You used to tell me how great it was to be with
             me—you wanted to make love all the time. But all of
             a sudden it's like it's dirty and you don't want me to
             get close at all.

EDWARD   That's not it.

DAVID   It is so. And I feel, you know, that without it there's
             nothing between us. And I thought there was a lot
             more.

EDWARD   David—

DAVID   I'm going to bed. And don't worry about her smelling
             the joint, I'll lean out the window to finish it.

             DAVID *exits.*

EDWARD   Shit.

             EDWARD *starts to wrap* EMMA's *birthday*
             present, an album of 78's. He stops, takes a
             record and puts it on an old phonograph.
             Fred Astaire sings, "The Way You Look
             Tonight." In a few moments, EMMA *appears*
             in the doorway behind him. She is wearing
             her bathrobe. She stands quietly. She sings
             along. EDWARD *turns when he sees her.*

EMMA   "Just the way you look tonight." I think I saw that old
              movie once. "Top Hat."

EDWARD   "Swingtime."

EMMA   "Swingtime?" No, I never saw "Swingtime." I saw
              "Top Hat."

EDWARD   But you told me you saw "Swingtime."

EMMA   When did I ever tell you that?

EDWARD   When I was little. You played me the songs on the
              piano, told me the story.

EMMA   "Swingtime?" Nah, I never saw it.

EDWARD   Yes you did.

EMMA   I just saw Fred and Ginger once, and that was "Top
              Hat." (*listening*) That's not one of my records.

EDWARD   It was for your birthday. David and I found it in an
              antique store.

EMMA   Oh, I used to love those old pictures. Your father never
              much cared for them so they didn't mean a lot to me
              after we were married.

              They listen to the record. Then EDWARD
              takes the needle off.

EDWARD   Mom? Look. Mike told me about the time he found
              you out cold on the floor. And we know about the
              LeBlanc kids finding you on the beach.

EMMA   Oh, those crazy kids. I had my eyes closed for about
              ten seconds so they thought I was dead. They watch
              too much of that darn TV, that's their problem.

EDWARD   But you are having spells.

EMMA   Every little once in while I feel faint and doze off. It's nothing to get excited about. It's just something about air getting to my head. Not enough oxygen every once in a while the doctor says. It's fairly common for someone my age.

EDWARD   Do you think you should keep driving your car?

EMMA   Oh, I don't drive it much. Just down to the Co-op for groceries.

EDWARD   Maybe you should take a taxi.

EMMA   I will most certainly not bring my groceries home in a taxi—people would think I was on Welfare. Well, they would. You don't know what people in a small place like this are like.

EDWARD   I do so. They're like us.

       EDWARD *puts the record away.*

EMMA   Oh, I realize that I'm going to have to give up the car. (*pausing*) I want to tell you something I've been thinking. I never thought I'd hear myself say this, but, now, I don't think I can live in this old house any longer.

EDWARD   What?

EMMA   It's getting way too big for me. Now this afternoon I phoned and made an appointment to go and see the Eventide Home on Monday, and I'll get together a list of other places around we can go and look at while you're still here. I can't go to the one in town because it's all French and I wouldn't know what anyone was saying to me. I'll have to move away.

EDWARD   You're talking like you'll have to do this tomorrow.

EMMA   Do you know how much cultch I'll have to clear out of this place? I better get started darn quick.

EDWARD   What did the doctor really say?

EMMA   Are you saying I'm lying to you?

EDWARD   No. But I don't think you're telling me the whole truth either.

EMMA   Occasionally I faint. Period. And not so often as you care to think. You used to faint too, remember? On the school bus. Because you'd never eat your breakfast and then you'd head out the door and light up a darn old cigarette.

EDWARD   Don't talk about back then. We're talking about now. Here and now.

EMMA   (*pausing*) The truth of the matter is that I have to get away from here because it breaks my heart to live in this house without your father. I know the two of you didn't see eye to eye on things, but you do miss him, don't you? (*pausing*) Well, don't you? (*pausing*) You don't even miss him, your own father?

EDWARD   I'm sorry. I know how much you love him, and how much he loved you.

EMMA   And you! He loved you too!

EDWARD   I guess I even know that.

EMMA   You guess!

EDWARD   Yes, I guess. Because I never felt it, he never let me know it. So I don't believe it.

EMMA   You ungrateful, miserable child. (*pausing*) You didn't
              try hard enough.

EDWARD   Yes, I did, I did so. But when nothing I said or did
              ever pleased him, I gave up.

EMMA   You have no idea what pleased him. He loved you!

EDWARD   I'll never know that. I shouldn't have listened to you, I
              should have told him about me.

EMMA   You didn't want to tell him, you wanted to put him to
              the test. He was your father, he didn't need any test.
              He would have gone on loving you. But it would have
              broken his heart. But he would have gone on loving
              you no matter what!

MICHAEL   (*off, singing to the hymn tune "Christ the Lord is
              Risen Today"*)

              "Vyia Rodd is dead today.
              Hallelujah.
              Dadadadadadaday.
              Hallelujah."

                        MICHAEL *enters, drunk, white paint on his
                        clothes.*

EMMA   I didn't hear your car come in.

MICHAEL   That's because it's in the ditch.

EDWARD   In the ditch!

EMMA   Are you alright?

MICHAEL   I'm fine. I figured I shouldn't drive it anymore, so I
              put it in the ditch and walked home.

EMMA   From where?

MICHAEL   Jake's Corner.

EMMA   Oh, Michael.

EDWARD   Did you smash it up?

MICHAEL   No, it's fine. It's just off the road.

EMMA   You're drunk. You've been driving and you're drunk.

MICHAEL   Relatively speaking, I'm pretty sober.

EDWARD   Where the hell have you been?

MICHAEL   Celebrating. Listen, "Vyia Rodd is dead today, Hallelujah—"

EMMA   Michael!

MICHAEL   Come on, we've all been waiting for this for years.

EDWARD   How come you're all covered with paint?

MICHAEL   I've been painting.

EMMA   At this time of night?

MICHAEL   Yeah. The overpass. The straight stretch just past the bridge near the dead skunk. But you don't know about that. There's a dead skunk out there. You can't smell it on me, can you?

EMMA   No.

MICHAEL   Good. I think my car stinks though. Have to scrub that front wheel in tomato juice.

EDWARD   What were you painting?

MICHAEL   The straight stretch.

EMMA   You were painting the highway?

MICHAEL   Yeah. And the overpass.

EMMA   You could have got yourself killed!

EDWARD   What did you paint?

MICHAEL   I did the overpass first, so it's longer. It says, (*trying not to laugh*) "Vyia Rodd is Dead Today."

EMMA   You're kidding.

MICHAEL   And on the road it just says, "She's dead." But the letters are bigger. It would have been more except for the skunk.

EMMA   What will people think of you?

MICHAEL   What the hell do I care? They never thought much of me to begin with.

EMMA   Well, you didn't have to go make a public jackass out of yourself.

MICHAEL   You don't think it's funny?

EMMA &   No!
EDWARD

EMMA   Ed, let me go get something on and I'll drive you out and you can bring his car back.

EDWARD   No, you're not driving tonight.

DAVID *enters.*

MICHAEL   Hey, buddy!

DAVID   You just get back from a party?

MICHAEL   You betcha!

DAVID   What are you celebrating?

MICHAEL   The jeezly old witch is dead!

EDWARD   What are you trying to do, wake her up?

MICHAEL   Am I loud?

EDWARD   Yes, you're loud. You woke David up.

DAVID   No, he didn't. I wasn't asleep.

MICHAEL   See? Everything's fine.

EMMA   Fine? You've been drinking and driving, you put your car in the ditch, you've been painting things on overpasses, disgracing yourself—

MICHAEL   And I killed a skunk. Don't forget the skunk.

EMMA   I don't care about some darned old skunk. I care what people are going to say about you.

MICHAEL   I'm a big disappointment.

EMMA   Now that's not what I—

MICHAEL   A big friggin' disappointment.

EDWARD   Knock it off Mike!

MICHAEL   It's true. Isn't that right? Hey? (*to* DAVID) What do
          you think?

DAVID   How'd you kill the skunk?

MICHAEL   With my bare hands.

EMMA   David, do you drive?

DAVID   No, I don't.

EMMA   We have to go get Michael's car.

EDWARD   Mom, you're not driving.

MICHAEL   (*to* DAVID) I didn't kill it with my bare hands.

EDWARD   Pat and I'll go out first thing in the morning. Or I'll
          have to walk over tonight.

MICHAEL   I ran over it by accident. I was gonna bury it, then I
          thought, you can't bury two skunks in one day. That's
          bad luck or something. That fuckin' old bitch.

EMMA   I didn't care for Vyia Rodd either, but I won't let you
          go on like this. It's indecent.

MICHAEL   I couldn't give a shit!

EDWARD   Knock it off, Mike!

MICHAEL   Why, am I embarrassing? Am I being embarrassing?
          S'okay. They're gonna laugh anyway, Ed. They
          always did. Everybody's been laughing at me since
          the day I was friggin' born.

EDWARD   That's a load of crap.

MICHAEL   Ever since the day I went to school and friggin' Vyia held up my scribblers when I wrote stuff backwards. I didn't mean to do it. Four friggin' years of that. Jeez. Grade one, grade two, grade three, grade four.

         PAT *has entered quietly behind him.*

MICHAEL   "How come you're so stupid?" Four fuckin' years of that bitch sayin' "How come you're so stupid. Why can't you be smart like your brother?" and makin' everybody laugh at me cause I write stuff backwards.

EDWARD   Michael, stop.

MICHAEL   No! I hate her! I hate her! And everybody called me Mikey Bird, Mikey Bird cause I was so little and they wouldn't play with me cause I couldn't play anything. "Mikey Bird sti-nks, Mikey Bird sti-nks." And you all hated me cause I left the Monopoly game out in the rain and it got ruined cause I'm so stupid.

         PAT *comes up behind him.*

MICHAEL   And now she's dead and I should feel better cause I hate her so much but it's just the same, it's gonna be just the same.

PAT   (*touching his arm*) Mike—

MICHAEL   (*seeing her, pausing and shoving her hand away*) And you! You! I burnt the wedding pictures and buried them by the cesspool and I didn't love you either when we got married but Jesus Christ Almighty I sure as hell hate your friggin' guts now! Fuck yas all!

         MICHAEL *runs out. Pause.*

PAT   (*running after him*) Mike! Michael! (*exiting*)

> EMMA *starts after them. She stops.*
> EDWARD *goes to her.*

EDWARD   Mom.

EMMA   Is he going to be alright?

EDWARD   Come on, come on inside.

> EDWARD *takes* EMMA *into the house.*

*On the beach a few minutes later. There is
moonlight and the sound of waves.
MICHAEL is crouched on the sand, rocking.
He has been crying. PAT is standing about
eight feet behind him. She has just found him
and he does not know she is there. Pause. She
does not approach him.*

MICHAEL   Stupid face. Stupid face, stupid stupid stupid stupid...

PAT   Michael? Mike?

MICHAEL   (*without turning*) Go way!

PAT   I'm sorry.

MICHAEL   Big deal.

PAT   But—

MICHAEL   Doesn't matter.

PAT   Yes it matters.

MICHAEL   Doesn't, doesn't change a friggin' thing. Leave me.

PAT   I want you to listen to me.

MICHAEL   I said, go way.

PAT   You won't even hear me when I say I'm sorry.

MICHAEL   Why should I? You just wanna feel better. You just
want me to forgive you so you can feel better.

PAT   Mike.

MICHAEL (*pausing*) Why should you? Why should you get to feel any better? Why should you be able to get to sleep?

PAT I just—

MICHAEL You just nothing. You just do nothing. You just say nothing. Nothing to me, nothing!

PAT No!

MICHAEL You just keep going and leave me behind now. Please! Go!

PAT I have to talk to you.

MICHAEL Oh, yeah. I know. "I'm sorry, I'm sorry. I made a mistake. I'm sorry." I heard it, now go.

PAT You—

MICHAEL I always feel bad, but you had to come and make me feel worse. Go way!

PAT No!

MICHAEL How can you get so close to someone and then say it's a mistake? A mistake! A friggin' mistake. "I made a mistake, Michael. Mikey-Bird, I made a friggin' mistake."

PAT No, please don't.

MICHAEL Some mistake. Some friggin' mistake...You walkin' round that jeezly motel room crying your friggin' eyes out. "I'm sorry. I did a bad thing. I made a mistake. I'm sorry, I'm sorry, I'm sorry." And I had to sit there like a friggin' doorknob while you packed your stuff. Packed? Christ, you were barely unpacked. Some

MICHAEL	friggin' honeymoon. Some goddam jeezly friggin' honeymoon that was. I'm just lucky it wasn't a surprise.
PAT	What?
MICHAEL	A surprise, a surprise, you deaf? You know what did surprise me? Eh? You know when? I was surprised that friggin' night in P.E.I., that's when I was friggin' surprised…"Hey, you don't kiss like somebody's kid brother." I was surprised when you started telling everybody how much you loved me. "My best friend's brother, imagine that." That was the friggin' surprise.
PAT	I thought I did.
MICHAEL	But you didn't! But I wanted to believe it. I really did.
PAT	So did I.
MICHAEL	You just wanted to be in love with Ed's little brother. (*pausing*) All of a sudden we're getting married at the end of the summer and I'm gonna be part of something big and grown up and get out of this stupid place. But I didn't know what it felt like. How was I supposed to know what love felt like? I didn't know it wasn't love. So stupid I don't know anything. Why am I so terrible? Is it just because I was little and read everything backwards? Everybody always left me, they always left me alone.
PAT	No, Michael, no.
MICHAEL	Yes, did so. If somebody's with me it's cause the person they really want to be with is away. I wanted to play so bad, and the kids said I could if I took down my pants and ran across Vyia's backyard, and she saw me out her window and stuck me in a cupboard at school and gave me the strap.

PAT   (*quietly*) Oh, Michael...

MICHAEL   The only one who wanted to play with me was
Maurice Gallant and his sister cause Vyia hated him
too cause he was French. And I was with Maurice that
time in Grade Two when we were playing up in
Evan's Field and I saw the little man jump into a lilac
bush and disappear. Little man about a foot high, and
everybody said I was crazy 'cept for Maurice cause he
saw him too. We saw him clear as day. Me and
Maurice is playing at somethin' when I saw somethin'
move and I said, "Hey Maurice, lookit" and he looked
and there was that little man watching us. And stupid
Maurice had to go and chase him, and he jumped into
a bush and went away. And Mom acts like it was real
cute or somethin'. "Member that time you and that
Gallant kid thought you saw that little elf?" But it was
creepy really. And I make like it was a joke type a
thing, but it really happened. I saw him. I did. But
Maurice and I started pretendin' like it never
happened and stopped talkin' about it, and then we
stopped talkin' to each other.

> PAT *has moved to stand close to* MICHAEL
> *during his speech. She kneels down beside*
> *him.*

PAT   Stop.

> PAT *puts her arms around* MICHAEL.

MICHAEL   No!

> MICHAEL *jumps at her touch, spinning*
> *around, making* PAT *lose her balance. She*
> *falls on her back. There is a split second.*
> MICHAEL *hesitates, then he jumps on top of*
> *her, pins her to the ground.*

MICHAEL   I hate you I hate you I hate you!

              *She looks up at him terrified, and begins to
              struggle. He holds her fast and is about to
              hurt her. Really hurt her. Then he stops, takes
              his hands off her. He cannot look at her face.
              She lies very still.*

MICHAEL   I wanted to hurt you so bad. To hear something break
              inside you like a little bone nobody could see. No
              blood, no ambulance, just little broken stuff hiding
              inside. I'm so stupid, I'm so stupid, too stupid to
              friggin' live.

PAT   (*quietly*) No...

MICHAEL   I make myself so friggin' sick I don't know anything
              else anymore. Why did you touch me? Why'd you let
              me touch you back?

PAT   When?

MICHAEL   That night, that night on the beach! Why did you
              touch me?

PAT   Because I didn't want the summer to end.

MICHAEL   Right.

PAT   Because I wanted to stop loving Ed.

MICHAEL   And you can't, you friggin' can't—

              EDWARD *runs in and hauls* MIKE *off* PAT,
              starts fighting.

EDWARD   Leave her! Leave her!

> PAT *pulls herself away from them. The
> brothers roll on the sand, struggling. Finally*
> EDWARD *crawls on top of* MICHAEL.
> EDWARD *holds* MICHAEL'S *shoulders,
> shakes them violently.*

PAT   EDWARD! MICHAEL! STOP!

EDWARD   Jerk, you big jerk!

PAT   Stop, Ed, please!

> PAT *tries to haul* EDWARD *off* MICHAEL.

EDWARD   Pat!

MICHAEL   Leave me!

> EDWARD *holds* MICHAEL'S *head between
> his hands.*

EDWARD   What are you trying to prove?

MICHAEL   Get offa me!

> EDWARD *releases* MICHAEL'S *head.*

EDWARD   You're hopeless.

> EDWARD *gets up,* MICHAEL *stays on the
> sand.* EDWARD *turns to* PAT.

EDWARD   You okay?

PAT   No.

> EDWARD *turns back to* MICHAEL.

PAT   He didn't hurt me, I'm okay! Leave him alone.

EDWARD   (*pausing*) We've got to do something about the car.

PAT   The car?!

EDWARD   Yeah, the car.

MICHAEL   My car can stay there till it friggin' rusts.

EDWARD   But people will—

MICHAEL   I could give a friggin' care about people! I could give a flying—

EDWARD   For Mom's sake!

MICHAEL   Didn't she tell you she's leaving town, goin' off to a home? Who cares what this town thinks anyway? Nobody cares. Nobody gives a damn.

EDWARD   Only person you think of is yourself.

MICHAEL   Oh that's hot comin' from you.

EDWARD   I don't want Mom upset anymore.

            MICHAEL *gets up.*

MICHAEL   You the only one allowed to upset her now?

EDWARD   What's your problem? Just what the hell is your problem?

PAT   Edward, leave him alone.

EDWARD   Are you as crazy as he is?

PAT   Cool your jets.

EDWARD   He's beatin' your head in and you're on his side.

PAT   Lay off. Lay off me and lay off Michael.

EDWARD   Christ, I'll never figure you out. You must thrive on friggin' abuse.

PAT   Knock it off.

EDWARD   This clown tackles you, Mark screws around on you—what the hell is it with you anyway?

PAT   You know what it is with me.

EDWARD   No, tell me.

PAT   You.

EDWARD   Mike give me the keys—I'll walk over and get your car.

MICHAEL   Drop dead.

PAT   I can still see the look on Mom's face when we told them who was getting married.

EDWARD   Oh, Pat. Jesus.

PAT   You know damn well all I really wanted was you.

EDWARD   Oh Jesus, not now—

PAT   It's hardly a big surprise. Just because we never talked about it doesn't mean we all haven't known about it for years.

EDWARD   That was ages ago, it's all over.

PAT   Oh, what do you know? What the hell do you know? (*pausing*) I see your hair and it's the same hair I wanted to touch fifteen years ago.

EDWARD   Stop saying this, stop.

PAT   No. I can't stand it anymore. I saw you with David
                  and all I wanted to do was hurt you. For fifteen years
                  the both of us have been jealous as hell of
                  everybody—and what's the point?

EDWARD   (*pausing*) I hate this place.

MICHAEL   Then stop coming back once a year to suck up to it.

EDWARD   You're crazy.

MICHAEL   No, I'm not! And quit tellin' me I am. (*pausing*) I wish
                  you were dead.

EDWARD   Mike.

MICHAEL   You're so fulla shit, I'm surprised you can walk.

EDWARD   You wanna see me walk? Give me the keys and I'll
                  walk over to the corner, get your—

MICHAEL   Night before the wedding, the night before the friggin'
                  wedding, Dad comes into my room and asks me if I'm
                  sure I'm doin the right thing.

PAT   What?

MICHAEL   "I wanna have a little talk, now do you think you're
                  doing the right thing? Do you think marrying Patsy is
                  the right thing?" Whisperin' away, scared ta death
                  you'd hear'm. An I'm so stupid I think, but Ed won't
                  let it happen if it's wrong. Ed won't let it happen.

EDWARD   Dad said that?

MICHAEL   All you do is bitch about this town but you're scared
                  shitless people'll find out yer a queer. Dad's dead, and

MICHAEL   he knew anyway. Ya think he's stupid? (*pausing*) Both a them whisperin' ta me alla time—makes me nuts.

PAT   What did Mac say?

MICHAEL   That's all. Nuthin.

EDWARD   Nobody in this place comes right out and says anything.

MICHAEL   Especially you.

EDWARD   Me?

MICHAEL   Yeah, you. (*pausing*) When I got back from Vermont I didn't wanna talk to anybody. So Dad asked me if I wanted to go fishing, and we went off fishing for a couple of days. Hardly talked, didn't have to. I knew what he felt. But I don't have a clue about you.

EDWARD   (*pausing*) I kept coming back here. Comin' back here waitin' for somebody to say something—to say, you did okay, that's alright—you made a mistake, we all make mistakes. Just one time for Dad not to act like I've got the plague. He'd give me that look, he'd just come into the room like every move I made was wrong. (*pausing*) I keep dreaming about me walking down the stairs and he's at the bottom and I think, "The wrong stairs, I came down, the wrong stairs again," cause he's gonna say, "What's in your room Ed?" like I've got a big secret that scares me shitless up there. I can be dreaming about you or David, anything, then it all changes, and I think, "oh God it's the Dad thing again." And I keep coming back here waitin' for my friggin' old man to come down outta the sky and talk to me one time. But he never did and now it's never gonna happen. (*pausing*) I keep thinking about him in the hospital after his last stroke, waking up all confused, not knowing how he got

EDWARD   there. Sayin', "Where am I? Was I in a car accident?"
              And all I could think of was I'd just met David and I
              couldn't let any of them know. I just felt so
              pointless...I'm sorry, Mike, I'm sorry.

MICHAEL   (*pausing*) After he died, Mom gave me the keys to his
              safety deposit box. Ya know what was in it? His
              policy, which was worth shit, one of Gramma's old
              rings, and a bunch of pictures we made for him when
              we were kids. Old pictures we did on those old exam
              tablets, remember? All rolled up in an elastic.

EDWARD   I never ever thought I'd miss him.

PAT   I loved him. He was the first grown up who made me
              feel important.

MICHAEL   Why did you come back here?

PAT   Because I had no where else to go.

MICHAEL   What's that supposed to mean?

PAT   Just what I said. (*pausing*) I was pregnant when I
              found out Mark was cheating on me.

EDWARD   What?

PAT   I was pregnant and I knew I had to leave him. Just my
              luck, eh?...I had an abortion...It wasn't as bad as I
              thought it would be. Mark's sister came with me.

EDWARD   Where was he?

PAT   He was in Toronto, at a conference...I tried to tell my
              mother yesterday, but we just ended up having a big
              fight and I didn't. So I jumped in Arnie's car and
              drove down here.

EDWARD   What'd you fight about?

PAT   My old man. (*pausing*) Do you know what she said to me? She said, "Why do you have to look just like that useless father of yours? There's no escaping him as long as you're around." (*pausing*) This was the first place I wasn't made to feel like shit.

EDWARD   (*pausing*) You okay now?

PAT   I did the only thing I could do...Oh, boy—I wish to Christ I'd never quit smoking.

MICHAEL   I've got a joint.

PAT   No, it's not the same. Thanks, Michael, but it's not the same...Well, here we are again, just like old times, eh boys? Yowsa yowsa yowsa.

> *By this point, all three of them are sitting together on the sand.*

EDWARD   That summer was the worst summer of my life. I was so lonely and so horny and I needed you guys so much that I pretended no one could get hurt. I knew the wedding was wrong, but I didn't say anything. Worse than that, I was best man—best man, that's a joke...Dad drove me crazy all my life, but I'm just the same. I'm just the same as he was.

PAT   (*pausing*) We should go get Michael's car.

EDWARD   Yeah.

> *They don't move, just sit quietly for a moment.*

MICHAEL   It's late, it's after dark, and you're still playing with your friends. Dad's at the backdoor callin' you and

MICHAEL   you're hiding in the dark, and the kids are all goin'
"Free the bunch Ed, free the bunch." And I wanted to
be big like you. But we are. We're as big as Dad now.
As big as Dad.

The three sit quietly. Hold a long moment.

EMMA *and* DAVID *are in the sunporch. Two days later.*

EMMA   I made a pig of myself last night on that lobster.

DAVID   You only had one.

EMMA   Yes, but the size of it! Cripes Kate. Those weren't canners—they must've cost Mike a fortune.

DAVID   Now I can say I've had fresh lobster.

EMMA   And that's the only way to have it—right out of the sea. But lobster and birthday cake. I need to have my head examined. And all that flyin' around yesterday wore me out. I still can't get over how you and Mike went to the fish plant to get those without me knowing about it. Must be getting old and stupid...I hope you don't mind if I ask you a little question.

DAVID   What?

EMMA   It's really none of my business.

DAVID   Oh?

EMMA   From the way that Ed talks, your family's split up, is that right?

DAVID   Well, yeah...My father left when I was thirteen.

EMMA   That must be hard on a kid growing up.

       DAVID *shrugs, not knowing what to say.*

EMMA   Your mother must be very proud of you. I mean, your
            pictures and everything.

DAVID   Well, actually...

EMMA   She isn't?

DAVID   She's still hoping I'll go into advertising or real estate
            or something.

EMMA   You don't say.

DAVID   It's the one thing she and my father agree on. They
            hoped that art school was going to be a phase.

EMMA   Well isn't that a shame? Not being excited by an artist
            in the family. Ed tells me your pictures are very good.

DAVID   He told you about them?

EMMA   Oh yes.

DAVID   I didn't think he'd talk to you about...you know, me.

EMMA   (*pausing*) Now tell me something. You two won't do
            something crazy like find some way-out minister and
            get married, will you?

DAVID   Um, I don't think so, no.

EMMA   Not that I don't think you people shouldn't be allowed
            to if you want—but, well, anything's possible with the
            United Church these days.

            Pause, then MICHAEL *enters.*

EMMA   They all packed yet?

MICHAEL	There's lots of time. Their plane doesn't leave for an hour and a half.

PAT enters with her bag.

EMMA	You got everything?
PAT	I think so.
EMMA	It's awful good of you to drive the boys to the airport.
PAT	Oh, it's on my way. More or less.
EMMA	It's gonna seem a little empty around here, isn't it Mike? Everyone off again.

MICHAEL grunts in agreement.

EMMA	It was good to have the house full of you kids.
DAVID	My camera. Excuse me.

DAVID exits.

PAT	Thanks for everything, Mom. I'll phone you before I leave Rexton.
EMMA	That'd be nice. And you never know, I just might surprise you one of these days and turn up out West to take a gander at that old mall.
PAT	You're on.

Pause.

MICHAEL	Want me to carry that to the car?
PAT	Oh, it's not heavy, Mike. It's—well, if you like. That'd be nice.

EMMA   Do you think your mother would like some of those rolls I made?

PAT   You don't have to do that.

EMMA   Oh, I made so many. Why don't I go wrap up a few for you to take up to her. Just take a second.

            EMMA exits. Pause, then MICHAEL clears his throat.

MICHAEL   Well. (*picking up her bag.*) All the best to you.

PAT   Thanks. Thanks, Michael.

            After an awkward second, MICHAEL formally extends his hand and she shakes it.

PAT   And to you.

            MICHAEL exits to car with PAT'S suitcase. DAVID enters with his camera, picks up his knapsack. EDWARD is behind him with luggage.

DAVID   That's not fair! (*to PAT*) Is there any way that we can see that Magnetic Hill on the way to the airport?

EDWARD   You don't want to see Magnetic Hill, God.

PAT   Sorry, kiddo, it's not on the way at all.

EDWARD   See? Thank you Pat.

PAT   But if I drive out to the highway from the far side of town, I can stop at the Take Out so you can take a picture of Ed beside the giant chicken.

DAVID   Ha! It's a deal! (*to EDWARD*) Gotcha!

EDWARD   Terrific.

DAVID   Oh, I want to get a picture of Michael by himself.
            Michael?

            David exits after MICHAEL.

EDWARD   Aren't you cute?

PAT   I do my bit.

EDWARD   Oh, Patty, what an I going to do?

PAT   Your asking for advice from the woman who's on her
            way to Mom and Aunt Horna's?

EDWARD   I hope it goes okay up in Rexton.

PAT   I'll take my sisters' kids to the beach, it'll be fine. Just
            a couple more days anyway—I'll be back in
            Edmonton by the end of the week...Look, if you're
            crazy over this guy...

EDWARD   Yeah?

PAT   Go for it. If you don't, you'll kick yourself and be
            miserable. If you do and it doesn't work out, you'll be
            more miserable. But if you do, and it works out...who
            knows, Eddie?

            EMMA *enters with rolls in a plastic bag.*

EMMA   An even dozen. Just to let her know I'm thinking of
            her.

PAT   Oh, thanks, Mom.

MICHAEL   (*entering*) Car's locked.

PAT   Hang on.

               PAT *and* MICHAEL *exit to the car.*

EMMA   Do you still take all those slides of paintings for your
               gallery?

EDWARD   Yes, why?

EMMA   Well, now, it's just that if you have any of David's,
               would you send me down a couple? I'd like to have a
               look at them.

EDWARD   Yeah? Sure, I can send you something.

EMMA   I probably won't know what they're about, but I'd like
               to see them.

               EDWARD *and* EMMA *walk towards the car.*

EDWARD   Sure...Now, you'll let me know when you find a place
               to move to that you like.

EMMA   We will. Mike and I'll keep you posted.

               MICHAEL *enters.*

EMMA   Won't we?

MICHAEL   What?

EMMA   Keep him posted.

MICHAEL   I guess. David wants to take your picture with Pat.

EMMA   He wants to take a picture of me?

PAT   (*off*) Come on, Mom.

EMMA   Oh, alright. But I bet my hair looks something awful.
              (*exiting*)

MICHAEL   I'll let you know how she's doing.

EDWARD   Thanks, thanks a lot. And David was serious, you
              know. Come on up and visit.

MICHAEL   (*shrugging*) Never know.

DAVID &   (*off*) Mike!
PAT

MICHAEL   Oh, Christ, I hate pictures.

              MICHAEL *exits towards the car.* EDWARD
              stays back and looks at the house a moment.
              DAVID *enters.*

DAVID   Come on, Edward, I want you in this too.

EDWARD   You won't have any film left over for the giant
              chicken if you're not careful.

DAVID   I've got a whole other roll.

EDWARD   You would.

DAVID   (*pausing*) I'm coming back to your place with you.

EDWARD   Um…

DAVID   I know you said you wanted to be by yourself, but—

EDWARD   David, I'm not ready to live together.

DAVID   What then? You want to go on dating forever?

EDWARD   No, but…

PAT   (*off*) Come on you two! We can't stand around here all day!

EDWARD   Hold your horses!

DAVID   (*pausing*) Ed?

EDWARD   (*pausing*) I'm so crazy, I'm so crazy that I thought if somebody loved you back it would be a solution, you know and...

DAVID   And what?

EDWARD   It isn't.

DAVID   (*pausing*) Your mother asked me if we were getting married.

EDWARD   You're kidding.

DAVID   I said we hadn't planned on it.

EDWARD   Good. Thank you. Get married, oh my God, Mother. She's probably worried about which one of us would wear white.

PAT   (*off*) ED!

DAVID   Let's talk when we get back to Toronto, okay?

PAT   (*off*) David, get him over here!

EDWARD   Let's go.

EDWARD *touches* DAVID'S *arm. They exit.*

EMMA *and* MICHAEL *are walking slowly on the beach.*

EMMA   Let me give you some money towards that lobster.

MICHAEL   No.

EMMA   But that was expensive, Michael. You didn't have to do that.

MICHAEL   I felt like it.

EMMA   But—

MICHAEL   Keep your stupid money.

EMMA   You're very good to me.

MICHAEL   (*pausing*) Did you like that helicopter?

EMMA   Well, you know me. I'm not the sort of person who'll even get on a merry-go-round. When it whisked us right up over the fairgrounds and saw those rides gettin' smaller and smaller down there, I started to get dizzy.

MICHAEL   You didn't like it?

EMMA   I didn't say that. Just took some getting used to, that's all. It was wonderful present. All my presents were wonderful presents. (*pausing*) I'm not going to sell the old house. Now that doesn't mean I expect you to go on living there if you don't want to. Young people need their own places. I know, cause I never had mine when I was young. But the Old Girl's lived here all her life now and packing up to move would probably

EMMA   just finish me off. So why not wait a few more years
              and just go from here? And I want to be where I used
              to be with your father. I can still feel the Old Fella
              around here. It wouldn't be the same at a senior
              citizens.

MICHAEL   No.

EMMA   Maybe I can get one of those V.O.N.'s

MICHAEL   Maybe.

EMMA   They must come in English.

MICHAEL   I'm going to winterize my place.

EMMA   Good.

MICHAEL   Think I'll drive up to Rexton next week, see Pat's
              brother about that generator.

EMMA   Good. You and Arnie got along real well. It's a shame
              not to keep up. (*pausing*) I looked for Rexton when I
              was up there.

MICHAEL   Up where?

EMMA   In the whirly-bird.

MICHAEL   Oh.

EMMA   Couldn't find it.

MICHAEL   No?

EMMA   Couldn't even find the town at first. Well, he flew us
              off Downshore and Old Stupid here, I didn't even
              know where we were till David pointed out the lobster
              factory and I got my bearings from that. There were

EMMA   just so many trees—miles and miles and miles of
trees—I guess I just never think about how big the
woods are still. And the craziest thing, I thought this
must be how the old MicMacs and settlers first saw it,
looking down at it all wild with woods full of
ponds—real swift thinkin' that...Then he took us out
on a big turn out over the Strait and we came in
towards the town from over the island. Sailboats all
over, and the Bay was so pretty blue—you could look
straight down through the water to the sandbars off
shore. But the town looked so small on the shore
beside all those woods, just nestled in there like a little
haven. And then, as soon as I thought I could see the
roof of the house down there in the maples, that darn
pilot started to fly us away from the town and towards
the Cape. But young David, he says something to the
pilot in French, and the next thing I knew they had
that helicopter turned around and we were flying
lower. And then, boys oh boys, it just seemed like we
were standing still, just hanging there looking down
on that old house. It looked exactly the way it looks in
dreams, you know, the kind where you're out in the
backyard and suddenly you remember that you know
how to fly. Then the pilot said something in French,
and David told me that he was saying what a beautiful
old house it was, so I said "thank you." And then I
saw you come out the back door and stand on the
porch. David touched my hand and pointed to you.
Then the back door opened again and Edward and Pat
were down there with you, and the three of you were
all looking up and waving at us. And David and the
pilot were talking in French again, and I didn't know
what they were saying, so all I could say was "thank
you." I just kept saying "thank you." That's all I could
think of to say.

Fade to black.

The End